20
BEST SMALL GARDENS

Tim Newbury

CASSELL
ILLUSTRATED

First published in the United Kingdom in 1999 by
Ward Lock

Reprinted 2000, 2002, 2006

This paperback edition first published in 2001 by
Cassell Paperbacks, Reprinted in 2006 by Cassell Illustrated
a division of Octopus Publishing Group Limited
2-4 Heron Quays, London, E14 4JP

Distributed in the United States of America by
Sterling Publishing Co., Inc.
387 Park Avenue South,
New York, NY 10016-8810

A CIP catalogue record for this book is available
from the British Library

ISBN-13: 978-1-841881-27-0
ISBN-10: 1-841881-27-9
10 9 8 7 6 5 4 3 2 1

Printed and bound in Hong Kong

Contents

Introduction

What is a small garden? There is no simple answer to this, of course, because what is small to one person could be enormous to another. The definition will, for example, depend on the owner's experience of gardening. A novice may find that a plot measuring about 10 × 13 metres (30 × 40 feet) is quite large enough to provide a challenge for their limited knowledge and resources. A more experienced gardener, on the other hand, might not be satisfied with anything less than a tenth of a hectare (a quarter of an acre) – roughly eight times larger – and might yearn to have even more space.

As building land becomes less readily available, however, the average size of gardens, especially those of new houses, is becoming smaller, and a plot that measures 10 × 13 metres (30 × 40 feet) is now typical, although by no means the smallest that may be found.

One of the secrets of success in designing a small garden is to make the best possible use of the limited area. Careful forward planning and organization are essential if the various elements of the garden are not only to be fitted into the available space but are to be arranged in a way that prevents them from appearing cramped and from being impractical. All the available space should be put to the best possible use, and features that can serve more than one purpose should, if necessary, be included. Wherever possible,

unnecessary complexity should be avoided: a golden rule is to keep the design simple and uncluttered. Use only a limited range of materials and, where practicable, repeat a colour, a material or even a shape in different parts of the garden.

Having a small garden invariably means that neighbouring gardens – and houses – are that much closer, and so the treatment of boundaries, such as fences, walls and hedges, takes on a much greater significance than in a larger garden, where a shrub border and a large tree or two can act as a screen. You will also have to consider carefully the position and type of any trees that are growing in adjoining gardens, bearing in mind that you will have little or no control over their siting and development. Your plans will have to include an assessment of the shadow patterns of deciduous trees in summer when they are in full leaf and also the potential shadows that will be cast when such trees have reached maturity.

Another important factor allied to the proximity of boundaries is being able to identify those parts of the garden where the microclimate is suitable – or unsuitable – for particular needs or purposes. A patio, for example, ideally needs to be located in a part of the garden that is sunny for much of the day. In a large garden a substantial section of the plot might receive the sun for most of the day, and the patio could be sited almost anywhere within this area. In a small garden, however, neighbouring buildings and boundaries might mean that the area of garden that is in sun for most of the day is quite restricted, and a patio would have to be carefully positioned to make the most of the available sun yet not be overlooked.

In a limited area certain elements can be scaled down to suit the reduced space – a small pool or water feature, for example, can be just as attractive as its larger counterpart – but some features, especially the patio, cannot be scaled down, simply because

◀ Careful initial planning and organization can produce a small garden that is full of interest and surprises, yet practical and uncluttered.

▶ Small trees such as this laburnum (*Laburnum anagyroides*) are doubly useful – pleasing in their own right and support for climbers like honeysuckle (*Lonicera* spp.)

they need a certain minimum area if they are to work properly, regardless of the size of the overall garden. You might find, therefore, that once you have planned the larger 'fixed' elements – patio, lawn, shed, play area and so on – the amount of space left for planting is restricted. This will affect your choice of planting in two ways. First, you will need to think very carefully about whether to use plants, especially trees and large shrubs, that may quickly outgrow their allotted space and cause problems both to you and, possibly, your neighbours. Your selection may have to be limited to dwarf or slow-growing varieties or those that can be easily clipped and pruned to keep to manageable proportions.

The second way your planting will be influenced by the available space is in the number of individual plants that can be physically grown in a limited area.

Plants that provide long periods of interest in the form of flowers, foliage or fruit and berries will be especially valuable, as will those with distinctive shapes and habits of growth.

One advantage of small gardens, particularly those that are very enclosed, is that they can be more sheltered, and therefore relatively warmer, than larger ones. The growing season in such a garden may well be extended by several weeks, and you may be able to grow choicer and more unusual plants than would be possible in a larger, more exposed plot.

Another advantage of having a small garden is, of course, the cost. Designing and building the features for a limited area is likely to be a much more realistic undertaking from the point of view of a budget than attempting something on a very much larger and grander scale.

It is clear, therefore, that small gardens present their owners with challenges and opportunities that are not always found to the same extent in larger gardens. The 20 individual designs in this book, while exhibiting a mixture of garden styles and shapes, have one factor in common: they are specifically for small gardens. Each design has been devised to take account of all the pitfalls and opportunities to be found within a modest plot. The designs illustrate how it is possible to make the best use of all the available space, and they use carefully selected plant combinations to provide the maximum amount of interest and effect with a limited range of varieties.

Each design combines functional areas – patios, lawns, play areas and so on – with more ornamental ones and at the same time ensures, by avoiding conflict and congestion, that the garden is a complete entity.

The designs need not be followed slavishly, of course, nor need they be copied in their entirety, although this could, with only minor modification, be achieved quite easily. They are intended to provide ideas for the owners of all small gardens. There may be individual features or solutions to practical problems of planning that would enable you to make better use of the space in your own garden. Ideas from different gardens – the use of trellis screening as a windbreak or an unusual selection of border plants for year-round colour, for example – could be combined into an entirely new scheme or could be adapted to fit into an existing garden.

Each of the 20 main designs is accompanied by two thumbnail sketches to demonstrate how a particular garden and its features can be re-arranged to suit plots of a different shape. Because the thumbnail sketches show the basic features – patio, lawn, borders, garden buildings and so on – in simple, outline form, they can be used as a basis for planning other styles of garden. They should not be regarded simply as alternatives to the particular type of garden they accompany.

Above all, this book demonstrates what it is possible to achieve in a small garden. Its aim is to inspire you to look at your own garden with fresh eyes and to see the potential it has, no matter what its size.

▲ Overhead structures add an extra dimension to gardens. The simple design and dark colour of this pergola are a perfect contrast to the busy, colourful planting.

◀ Garden buildings and other unattractive structures can be difficult to hide in very small gardens. One solution is to make a positive feature out of them instead.

Modern Garden

The design

The effectiveness of this modern garden design results from the combination of a bold, geometric ground plan; simple, restrained planting that shows off plants to their best effect; and the use of ornamental features and materials that are attractive both individually and in combination with each other. Circular themes are particularly valuable in helping to disguise awkwardly shaped spaces, such as this wide, shallow plot, especially when the straight lines and corners of the boundaries can be masked or softened by planting. A central circle of lawn is echoed in two pools and by the paving that encloses it, which leads from a small patio by the house to a seat beneath a tree.

The longest views in the garden are diagonally from corner to corner, and placing features in each of these corners creates focal points that direct attention away from the long, straight boundary beyond the lawn. This design is not only successful because of its appearance, however, because there is ample space – in a comparatively small garden – for outdoor relaxation. The extra width of the plot means that a very useful and practical utility area can be tucked away behind a hedge at the left-hand side.

This striking outdoor room relies on defined structure and the crisp lines of the decking for effect. Plants are used as a soft, green contrast.

The planting

The planting can be divided into two types. First, there is the planting that softens and disguises the straight, square boundaries, at the same time acting as a background to the garden features. Second, plants are used as individual features in their own right to be appreciated for their form, flowers or foliage.

Background planting consists of a conifer hedge (*Thuja plicata* 'Atrovirens'), which separates and screens off the utility area and the shed, while the two remaining boundaries are planted with ivy (*Hedera hibernica*, syn. *H. helix* subsp. *hibernica*) and Boston ivy (*Parthenocissus tricuspidata* 'Veitchii'), both of which are bold leaved and will quickly cover the garden walls. At the base of these, low informal hedges of *Fuchsia magellanica* 'Versicolor' and *Rosa* 'Surrey' (syn. *R.* 'Korlanum') disguise the junction between the horizontal paved areas and the vertical walls – both of these varieties flower over a long period for added interest.

Individual feature plants are deliberately limited in choice – *Photinia serratifolia* (syn. *P. serrulata*), box elder (*Acer negundo*), *Ceanothus* 'Italian Skies', black bamboo (*Phyllostachys nigra*) and Japanese angelica tree (*Aralia elata*), with a drift of regal lilies (*Lilium regale*) to provide dramatic flowers and scent close to the patio.

This planting will require virtually no maintenance other than light, late-winter trimming and dead-heading of the roses and cutting back the fuchsias in early spring to ensure low, bushy growth with lots of flowers later on. Plant individual fuchsias about 60cm (2ft) apart). The thuja hedge is less vigorous than the ubiquitous Leyland cypress (× *Cupressocyparis leylandii*) and will require only an annual trim in early spring to keep it in shape; individual thujas should be planted at a distance of 45cm (18in) to create a good hedge. It is also far more suitable for a small garden because it can be easily kept at a modest height of 1.5–1.8m (5–6ft).

PLANTING PLAN

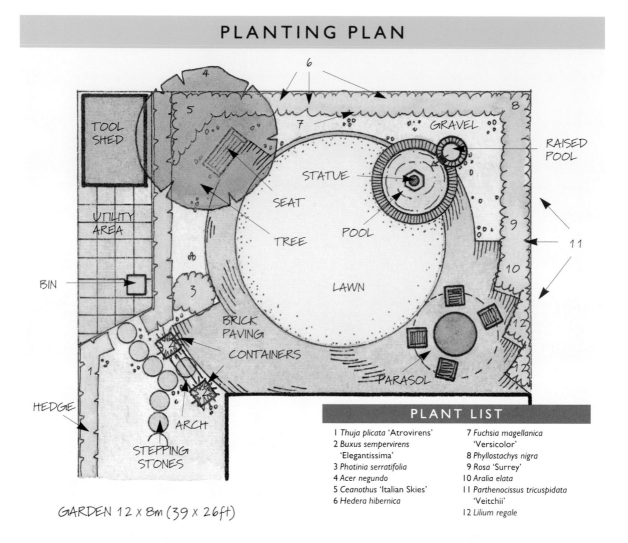

GARDEN 12 x 8m (39 x 26ft)

PLANT LIST

1 *Thuja plicata* 'Atrovirens'
2 *Buxus sempervirens*
  'Elegantissima'
3 *Photinia serratifolia*
4 *Acer negundo*
5 *Ceanothus* 'Italian Skies'
6 *Hedera hibernica*

7 *Fuchsia magellanica*
  'Versicolor'
8 *Phyllostachys nigra*
9 *Rosa* 'Surrey'
10 *Aralia elata*
11 *Parthenocissus tricuspidata*
  'Veitchii'
12 *Lilium regale*

The features

The circular lawn is the pivot around which the rest of the garden revolves, and its shape is therefore carefully picked out with an edging of dark brick, which also acts as a mowing strip. For hard wear, the turf mix includes a dwarf perennial rye grass, but this could be replaced with finer leaved varieties of hard fescue and browntop bent if use is likely to be very light or occasional.

Around the lawn terracotta-coloured brick paving links the various parts of the garden and provides

sitting areas. The bricks for this paving are laid in a stretcher bond, forming concentric circles with the lawn edge. Beyond the paving the ground is covered with cream-coloured gravel or limestone chippings, which continues underneath the perimeter plants. The simplicity of the design means that — apart, obviously, from the lawn, pools and brick paving — all the garden can be easily mulched with a porous, weed-suppressing fabric, with the plants planted through holes cut in it and the gravel laid on top.

The two pools continue the circular theme. The lower and larger of the two is made from a flexible liner and is edged in the same dark brick as the lawn. The upper one, which is raised by about 45cm (18in), is built entirely of this brick, rendered inside with waterproofed mortar, and with a cascade made from a thin piece of stainless steel directing water down into the large pool, in the centre of which stands a black metal statue on a white plinth.

Beneath the box elder is a white-painted garden seat, placed on an extension to the brick paving. The colour of the seat is in complete contrast to the black wrought-iron arch that stands at the entrance to the garden and that is flanked on either side by topiary specimens of variegated box (*Buxus*

sempervirens 'Elegantissima'). The white theme and style of the garden seat are repeated in the chairs and table on the patio, which is screened from the sun by a large fabric parasol.

The utility area, which is hidden away from sight behind the thuja hedge, is very simple. It is laid out with economical square concrete flagstones and provides space for a plain self-assembly shed for storing garden tools, bicycles and so on. There is also room for refuse and compost bins if required, and a path of circular, terracotta-coloured concrete stepping stones laid in the white gravel links the garden with this utility area and the front of the house.

VARIATIONS

▶ Triangular variation

The pool is pulled back to the edge of the lawn, making more effective use of the point of the apex of the triangular plot. Repositioning the arch creates a gateway into the utility area behind the hedge.

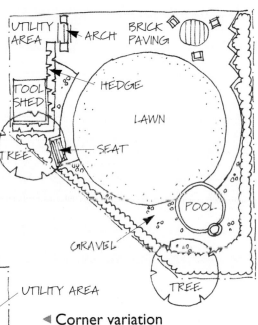

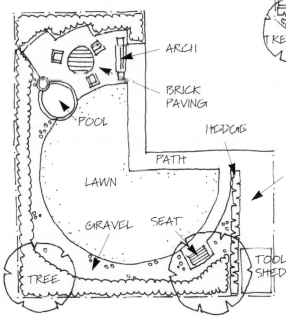

◀ Corner variation

The lawn is made wider by wrapping it around the corner of the house, to provide a link between both ends of the garden. Placing another tree in the far corner creates an additional focal point.

Gravel Garden

The design

One of the disadvantages of a very small garden is the fact that the space remaining after you have allocated areas for planting, paving and other features is often too small or awkward to be of practical use for a lawn. In such a garden it is, therefore, often far better to cover the ground with gravel or chippings or even bark if a softer surface is preferred.

The design of this small garden not only replaces grass areas with gravel – which is also relatively economical – but also cleverly hides the fact that it is, in fact, square by using curving and staggered paths, generous perimeter planting and a succession of focal points and features.

From the patio a circuitous route around the garden leads through a series of changing views and aspects, culminating in a tiny gazebo tucked away behind a small tree before rejoining the patio. Interest in such a small space is provided not only in the foreground by a water feature but also in the middle distance by arches and a statue, and finally, by planting in front of the boundary fencing. The overall style of the garden is informal, with the materials and planting being carefully selected to blend naturally with each other and to provide an abundance of interest, which successfully diverts attention away from the small dimensions and shape of the plot.

The planting

A common characteristic of small, enclosed gardens is that they can often be very warm and sheltered and, depending on their aspect and soil type, sometimes quite dry as well. Wherever possible, planting in any garden should take advantage of such physical limitations, and to that end the planting in this particular situation includes many plants that will tolerate – or indeed thrive – in drier, well-drained and protected situations.

Framework planting is vital in all gardens, and here large shrubs – such as choisya, Moroccan broom (*Cytisus battandieri*), deutzia, viburnum, weigela and mahonia – and climbers – such as potato vine (*Solanum jasminoides*), trumpet vine (*Campsis radicans* f. *flava*), clematis, roses and jasmine – on the boundary walls and trained up the arches do just that. While the main flowering season is from spring to autumn, there is still sufficient evergreen foliage and stem interest during the winter period to make this an attractive garden at any time of the year.

An added attraction, and one that is particularly welcome in a small garden, is scent, and there are several plants here that provide this through their flowers or foliage, including *Clematis armandii* 'Apple Blossom', rock rose (*Cistus ladanifer*), fennel (*Foeniculum vulgare* 'Giant Bronze') and lavender (*Lavandula angustifolia* 'Munstead' and *L. stoechas* subsp. *pedunculata*).

Trees always add an extra dimension of height and scale, but care must be taken in choosing one for such a small space so that it does not become an embarrassment. In this example a golden Indian bean tree (*Catalpa bignonioides* 'Aurea') is a good choice. A relatively modest tree, it can still be pruned quite hard if required, and this will also stimulate it to produce larger, brighter gold leaves. In the opposite corner, *Sorbus fruticosa* 'Koehneana' is rarely more than a very large shrub or a very small tree, and is therefore ideally suited for a restricted space with its light foliage and masses of white autumn berries.

The features

A generous patio of random, rectangular York flagstones is angled to face into the diagonally opposite corner of the garden, and it is laid with an irregular outline, which contrasts with the straight lines of the boundary fence. The joints of the paving are left unpointed and are filled with fine grit,

Gravel is a good mulch and an ideal foil for many small plants, particularly sun lovers such as fescue (*Festuca glauca*) and valerian (*Centranthus ruber*).

PLANTING PLAN

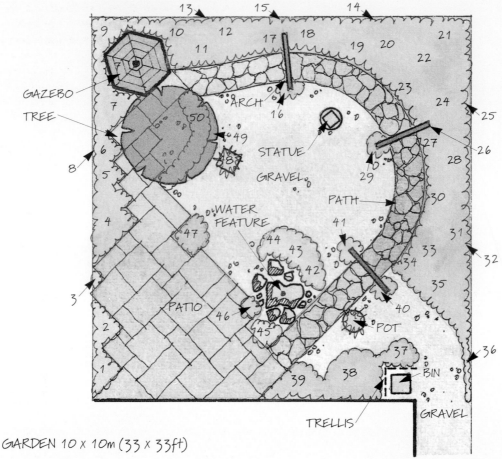

GAZEBO

TREE

ARCH

STATUE

GRAVEL

WATER
FEATURE

PATH

PATIO

POT

BIN

TRELLIS

GRAVEL

GARDEN 10 x 10m (33 x 33ft)

PLANT LIST

1 *Choisya* 'Aztec Pearl'
2 *Phygelius capensis*
3 *Solanum jasminoides*
4 *Agapanthus* 'Bressingham White'
5 *Olearia × haastii*
6 *Phormium tenax*
7 *Berberis thunbergii* 'Silver Beauty'
8 *Campsis radicans* f. *flava*
9 *Cytisus battandieri*
10 *Deutzia × kalmiiflora*
11 *Lavandula angustifolia* 'Munstead'
12 *Berberis × lologensis* 'Apricot Queen'
13 *Schizophragma hydrangeoides*
14 *Clematis armandii* 'Apple Blossom'
15 *Rosa* 'Meg'
16 *Clematis macropetala* 'Markham's Pink'
17 *Heuchera* 'Rachel'

18 *Spiraea thunbergii*
19 *Gaillardia* 'Kobold'
20 *Cotinus coggygria* 'Royal Purple'
21 *Sorbus fruticosa* 'Koehneana'
22 *Foeniculum vulgare* 'Giant Bronze'
23 *Helichrysum* 'Schwefellicht'
24 *Viburnum tinus* 'Eve Price'
25 *Celastrus orbiculatus* Hermaphrodite
  Group
26 *Rosa* 'Schoolgirl'
27 *Nepeta × faassenii*
28 *Mahonia × media* 'Lionel Fortescue'
29 *Jasminum polyanthum*
30 *Platycodon grandiflorus* var. *albus*
31 *Clematis* 'Lady Northcliffe'
32 *Rosa* 'New Dawn'
33 *Cistus ladanifer*

34 *Euphorbia × martinii*
35 *Lavandula stoechas* subsp. *pedunculata*
36 *Trachelospermum jasminoides* 'Variegatum'
37 *Viburnum tinus* 'French White'
38 *Weigela* 'Florida Variegata'
39 *Kniphofia* 'Little Maid'
40 *Lathyrus odoratus*
41 *Clematis alpina*
42 *Tsuga canadensis* 'Jeddeloh'
43 *Stipa gigantea*
44 *Helianthemum* 'Rhodanthe Carneum'
45 *Hebe* 'Purple Elf'
46 *Helictotrichon sempervirens*
47 *Viburnum japonicum*
48 *Cordyline australis* Purpurea Group
49 *Catalpa bignonioides* 'Aurea'
50 *Parahebe lyallii*

allowing small plants such as thyme (*Thymus serpyllum*) and biting stonecrop (*Sedum acre*) to colonize.

Around the garden, linking each end of this patio, is a narrow path constructed from random pieces of York stone laid in crazy-paving style. The joints between the pieces of stone in this case need to be pointed with a sand–cement mortar to provide adequate strength and cohesion.

Over the path are three delicate, round-topped, black, wrought-iron arches, which provide support for a mixture of suitable climbers. These arches are not parallel to each other, and a different view is framed as you walk beneath each one.

At the junction of the path and the far corner of the patio is a small, hexagonal, wrought iron gazebo, made in the same style and colour as the arches. This straddles a York flagstone base and beneath it is a small seat, somewhat screened from view by the catalpa and therefore affording some privacy from the rest of the garden.

In the foreground, at the start of the path, is a water feature consisting of a large rock, which is

drilled to take a pipe leading from a concealed water tank and submersible pump set in the ground beneath it. Water emerges in a gentle bubbling flow. The beauty of this type of fountain is that it is virtually maintenance-free and, probably more importantly, is safe for gardens where there are small children around.

The boundary fence is made of thin planks of wood that are nailed vertically to horizontal rails set between wooden or concrete posts in 'palisade' style and that are stained dark grey. This not only provides a secure boundary but is also a very effective backdrop to the planting. The same style of construction is used to create a lower screen around the refuse bin.

Finally, the gravel area in the centre of the garden is laid on top of a porous landscape fabric, which primarily acts as a weed-suppressant but also prevents the gravel from being trodden and mixed into the soil below, keeping it looking fresh and clean. It is, therefore, an excellent surface on which to stand pots, statues and other ornaments.

VARIATIONS

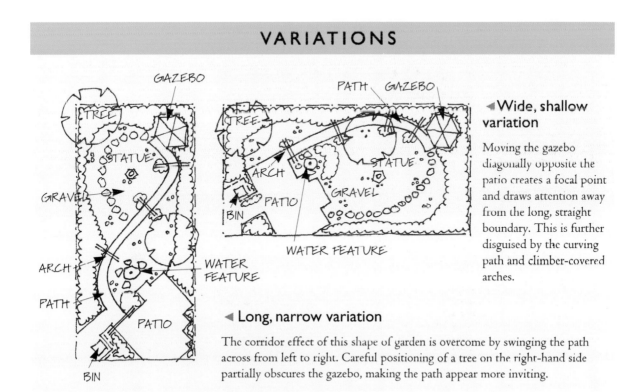

◀ Wide, shallow variation

Moving the gazebo diagonally opposite the patio creates a focal point and draws attention away from the long, straight boundary. This is further disguised by the curving path and climber-covered arches.

◀ Long, narrow variation

The corridor effect of this shape of garden is overcome by swinging the path across from left to right. Careful positioning of a tree on the right-hand side partially obscures the gazebo, making the path appear more inviting.

Shady Garden

The design

There are essentially two types of shade that need to be taken into account when you are designing a garden. The first of these is to be found immediately beneath the crown of trees or large shrubs, where the bulk of the light received by smaller plants beneath these crowns will come from the side rather than from directly above. To complicate matters further, these smaller plants will also have to compete with the vigorous root systems of the larger ones for both moisture and nutrients.

The second type is created when a solid object, such as a building or high fence, blocks out the sun from part of the garden by creating a shadow. This type of shadow is far less restrictive, however, because the plants sitting in this shadow will still, as a rule, receive light and moisture from above.

This particular example deals with both types of shadow. Not only is the garden north-facing so that the sunniest part is at the far end, furthest from the house, but in the gardens on either side there are mature trees that overhang, so causing additional shade and root competition.

The design tackles these problems by locating the patio area and ornamental garden at the far end of the garden rather than in the more obvious place by

the house. Here, they will be away from the influence of the shadow cast by the building and out of the overhang of the neighbouring trees. As far as possible, all the utility areas – that is, the shed, bin store and compost heaps – are in the shadier part of the garden near the house, where the conditions will not affect their usefulness, and they are separated from the ornamental garden by a lightweight trellis screen.

Two small sections of the ornamental garden are still partly overhung by the trees, so here the planting consists of varieties that are tolerant not only of some shade but also of the drier ground conditions that will be encountered there. This part of the garden is effectively a square, and the design for this area therefore relies on an almost semi-circular lawn with a curving path and an angled patio to divert attention away from its squareness and the straight boundaries.

The planting

In the ornamental half of the garden planting consists of an interesting mixture of shrubs, perennials and climbers to provide interest at all times of the year. Advantage is taken of the sun-trap at the far end, where sun-loving plants, such as *Trachelospermum asiaticum*, *Forsythia suspensa* (trained), *Ceanothus impressus* (trained) and *Philadelphus* 'Belle Etoile', are planted.

Immediately beneath the overhang of the existing trees, shade- and drought-tolerant plants have been selected. These include purple hazel (*Corylus maxima* 'Purpurea'), foxglove (*Digitalis purpurea* Excelsior Group) and Japanese anemone (*Anemone × hybrida* 'Honorine Jobert').

On the trellis screen deciduous climbers, such as honeysuckle (*Lonicera × tellmanniana*) and *Parthenocissus henryana* (syn. *Ampelopsis henryana*), are grown to provide summer screening when the sun is higher in the sky but allow light to pass through in the darker, shorter days of winter, when they are bare of leaves.

In the utility area, a central plot away from the influence of the neighbour's trees can be used to grow salad crops and other vegetables such as lettuce

PLANTING PLAN

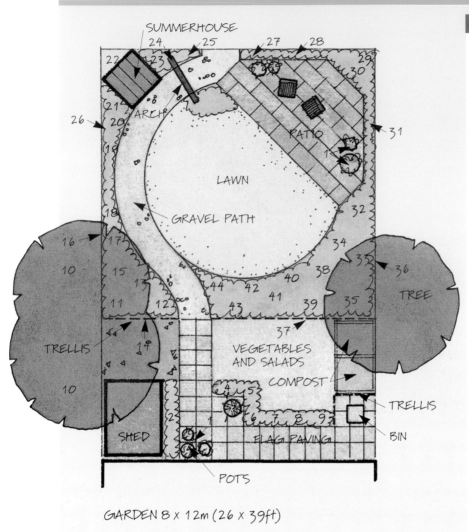

SUMMERHOUSE

ARCH

LAWN

GRAVEL PATH

PATIO

TREE

TRELLIS

VEGETABLES
AND SALADS

COMPOST

TRELLIS

BIN

SHED

FLAG PAVING

POTS

GARDEN 8 x 12m (26 x 39ft)

PLANT LIST

1 Annuals in containers
2 *Pyracantha* 'Soleil d'Or'
3 *Hosta sieboldiana* var. *elegans*
4 *Viburnum davidii*
5 *Anemone sylvestris*
6 *Euonymus fortunei* 'Sheridan Gold'
7 *Geranium phaeum*
8 *Skimmia japonica* 'Rubella'
9 *Astilbe* × *arendsii* 'Fanal'
10 Existing trees in neighbouring gardens
11 *Corylus maxima* 'Purpurea'
12 *Dryopteris erythrosora*
13 *Lamium maculatum* 'Chequers'
14 *Lonicera* × *tellmanniana*
15 *Digitalis purpurea* Excelsior Group
16 *Clematis* 'Beauty of Worcester'
17 *Crocosmia* × *crocosmiiflora*
18 *Campanula persicifolia*
19 *Spiraea japonica* 'Anthony Waterer'
20 *Hebe* 'Great Orme'
21 *Philadelphus* 'Belle Etoile'
22 *Amelanchier lamarckii*
23 *Rosa* 'Ballerina'
24 *Trachelospermum asiaticum*
25 *Pleioblastus auricomus*
26 *Rosa* 'Gloire de Dijon'
27 *Pyracantha* 'Orange Glow'
28 *Forsythia suspensa*
29 *Garrya elliptica* 'James Roof'
30 *Aster novi-belgii* 'Lady in Blue'
31 *Ceanothus impressus*
32 *Hydrangea arborescens* 'Annabelle'
33 *Ilex aquifolium* 'Aurea Marginata'
34 *Viola* 'Belmont Blue'
35 *Ligustrum japonicum*
36 *Clematis alpina* 'Columbine'
37 *Parthenocissus henryana*
38 *Anemone* × *hybrida* 'Honorine Jobert'
39 *Ribes sanguineum* 'Tydeman's White'
40 *Pulmonaria rubra* 'Redstart'
41 *Viburnum sargentii* 'Onondaga'
42 *Persicaria affinis* 'Donald Lowndes'
43 *Taxus baccata* 'Fastigiata Aurea'
44 *Hemerocallis* 'Stella de Oro'

and beans that do not require such a high level of sun for ripening as tomatoes or onions might need for example.

Separating the utility area from the paving immediately by the house is a small border of low plants, including *Viburnum davidii* and *Euonymus fortunei* 'Sheridan Gold', which will tolerate the shadier conditions here and also provide interest, particularly in winter.

The features

The semicircular lawn is the central feature around which the ornamental section of the garden revolves. It is edged with thin wooden boards, which are nailed to pointed stakes driven into the ground, and all the wood is treated with preservative beforehand to prevent it from rotting. This lawn edging also forms one side of the gravel path, which is retained on the other side with a similar edging. The gravel for the path is laid on a hardcore base that has been blinded with sand or crushed brick dust where the ground is soft. On firmer ground, however, it may be laid directly onto the soil, provided that any weeds or grass are first skimmed off and a mulching fabric is laid on top before it is finished off with the gravel. A tiny, square cedarwood summerhouse makes an ideal focal point in the corner of the garden at the end of the path, and a simple, matching cedarwood arch provides a hint of separation between the summerhouse and the patio in the adjacent corner, which consists of terracotta-coloured concrete flagstones. These give a warm effect, and they are laid in parallel lines to accentuate the angle of the patio to the boundaries.

The paving around the house is made up of concrete flagstones, with a textured finish to make them non-slip. This is particularly important where the sun cannot reach wet or icy patches in winter.

Around the boundary of the garden, a combination of a low brick wall surmounted by medium height trellis panels provides a degree of privacy yet still allows more light through than a solid wall or fence would. The same type of trellis, this time full height but without the wall, is also used to create the dividing screen across the garden, with lower, narrower panels around the refuse bin.

Beneath the overhanging trees, the otherwise difficult, dead space is usefully taken up by a small garden shed on one side of the garden, with a barked and membraned area in front of it for outdoor storage and two compost bins on the other side of the salad and vegetable plot.

VARIATIONS

▶ Square variation

The extra width of this shape means that the utility area and vegetable garden can be slotted into the corners, making extra room for a lawn, which is further helped by moving the summerhouse to the corner immediately behind the patio.

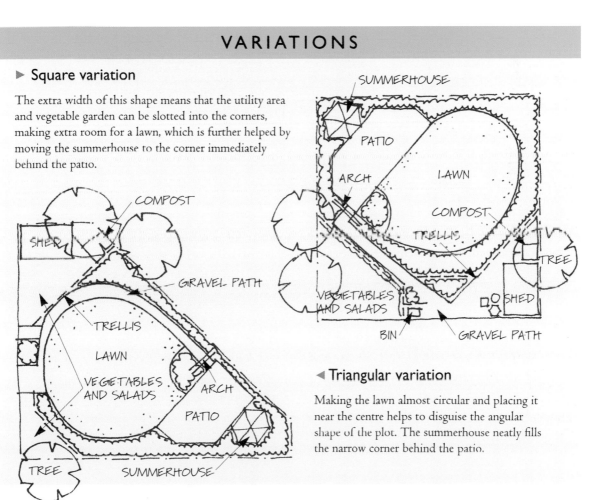

◀ Triangular variation

Making the lawn almost circular and placing it near the centre helps to disguise the angular shape of the plot. The summerhouse neatly fills the narrow corner behind the patio.

Family Garden

The design

Family gardens can sometimes be the most difficult to design, mainly because there is invariably not enough space – or would appear not to be – to accommodate all the features and functions that you would expect, or like, to see. This dilemma becomes even more apparent in a very small garden, such as this one, and it is therefore vital that all the space is put to good use.

Because of its shape this corner garden can be conveniently divided into four areas: a basic utility space with a small shed, refuse bin, fuel bunker and hard standing; an enclosed lawn, play area and brick paving, which is ideal for children and can be easily supervised at all times from the house; a generous patio for slightly more passive recreation; and a small vegetable garden, which even manages to squeeze in a greenhouse. These last three areas are all linked by a small pergola at the corner of the house, which acts as a pivot for the design as a whole.

With so much going on in such a small space there is always a danger that the garden will look bitty and piecemeal, and to counter this the design incorporates two strong themes. The first of these is the brick paving, which starts at the patio and continues right around the house to the entrance of the utility area. The second theme is the use of the same colour stain – in this case light oak – to treat all the woodwork in the garden. The only exception to this is the pergola, which, because of its importance in the overall design, is stained black to emphasize its presence.

The planting

In a family garden the main constraints likely to influence the style and detail of planting are cost, safety, durability and ease of maintenance. The relative importance of each of these will, of course, vary from family to family. In this example, the planting has been designed to use comparatively undemanding varieties that will, on maturity, provide good all-round interest and that are tolerant of a certain amount of abuse or damage. *Viburnum × bodnantense* 'Dawn', *Weigela florida* 'Foliis Purpureis' and red-barked dogwood (*Cornus alba* 'Spaethii') are shrubs that will regrow from a stump if they are cut back hard and that are quite forgiving of the odd football or frisbee. An element of evergreen planting extends the season of interest into winter as well as forming an essential part of the garden's structure. Plants for this purpose include variegated Portugal laurel (*Prunus lusitanica* 'Variegata'), holly (*Ilex aquifolium* 'Pyramidalis') and *Escallonia* 'Apple Blossom'.

Small front-of-border plants have been selected not only for their attractive flowers or foliage, but also for their effectiveness as ground cover. Day lily (*Hemerocallis* 'Burning Daylight'), black-eyed susan (*Rudbeckia fulgida* var. *deamii*) and cranesbill (*Geranium himalayense* 'Plenum') are ideal for this purpose.

The features

The patio and main paved areas around the house consist of brindled concrete paving bricks laid in basketweave style. Elsewhere in the vegetable garden and utility area, where appearance is not as critical, paving is kept to simple plain concrete flagstones in order to keep down costs.

Keeping the lawn a simple shape makes grass cutting easier, particularly if a mowing strip of treated wooden edging boards, as in this example, or bricks is used. This edge also helps to separate the grass from the play area, which is covered in a thick layer of chipped bark laid on top of a porous mulching membrane. The play area is partly enclosed by a trellis screen, stained in a light oak colour. All that would be needed to secure the area completely

Family gardens should ideally incorporate a range of features, but still leave plenty of open space for general play and relaxation.

would be an additional trellis panel and gate built into the side and one end of the pergola. This trellis screen also provides some protection to the back of a small greenhouse just inside the vegetable garden, with a robust evergreen shrub (*Elaeagnus pungens* 'Maculata') acting as a buffer at one end.

PLANTING PLAN

PLANT LIST

1 *Cotoneaster horizontalis*
2 *Hedera helix* 'Oro di Bogliasco'
3 *Brachyglottis greyi*
4 *Agapanthus* Headbourne Hybrids
5 *Viburnum* × *bodnantense* 'Dawn'
6 *Juniperus* × *pfitzeriana* 'Gold Coast'
7 *Hemerocallis* 'Burning Daylight'
8 *Miscanthus sinensis* 'Variegatus'
9 *Leucanthemum* × *superbum* 'Wirral Supreme'
10 *Jasminum nudiflorum*
11 *Weigela florida* 'Foliis Purpureis'
12 *Prunus lusitanica* 'Variegata'
13 *Lonicera periclymenum* 'Belgica'
14 *Ilex aquifolium* 'Pyramidalis'
15 *Clematis orientalis*
16 *Hedera helix* 'Glacier'
17 *Clematis* 'Ville de Lyon'

18 *Jasminum officinale* 'Aureum'
19 *Hydrangea anomala* subsp. *petiolaris*
20 *Hebe* 'Midsummer Beauty'
21 *Rosa* 'Zéphirine Drouhin'
22 *Clematis alpina* subsp. *sibirica* 'White Moth'
23 *Elaeagnus pungens* 'Maculata'
24 *Escallonia* 'Apple Blossom'
25 *Cornus alba* 'Spaethii'
26 *Philadelphus* 'Silberregen'
27 Herbs in containers
28 *Juniperus virginiana* 'Sulphur Spray'
29 *Hibiscus syriacus* 'Hamabo'
30 *Viburnum* × *globosum* 'Jermyns Globe'
31 *Rudbeckia fulgida* var. *deamii*
32 *Aster amellus* 'Rosa Erfüllung'
33 *Choisya ternata* 'Sundance'
34 *Geranium himalayense* 'Plenum'
35 *Scabiosa caucasica* 'Miss Willmott'
36 *Fuchsia magellanica* 'Versicolor'

GARDEN 12 x 14m (39 x 46ft)

A simple, bold design for the wooden, black-stained pergola makes it all the more effective as both a visual and physical link between the areas of garden and the dark stain sets off the various climbers admirably.

In the triangular space defined by the patio and the junction of the boundary fences, part of the space is taken up by a water feature consisting of a reproduction millstone through which water emerges in a gentle, bubbling flow, pumped up from a submerged tank directly beneath. Around the millstone is strewn a mixture of small boulders and sea-washed stone cobbles.

Small touches to complete the garden include a birdtable, which is set in the border behind the patio and can be seen from the house; a bench seat on the patio; and a collection of various pots and containers, also on the patio, planted with a selection of spring bulbs, flowering annuals and herbs for use in the kitchen.

VARIATIONS

► Rectangular variation

The more regular proportions of this garden allow the efficient use of space, with the patio opening straight onto the lawn. The angled layout draws the eye from any squareness.

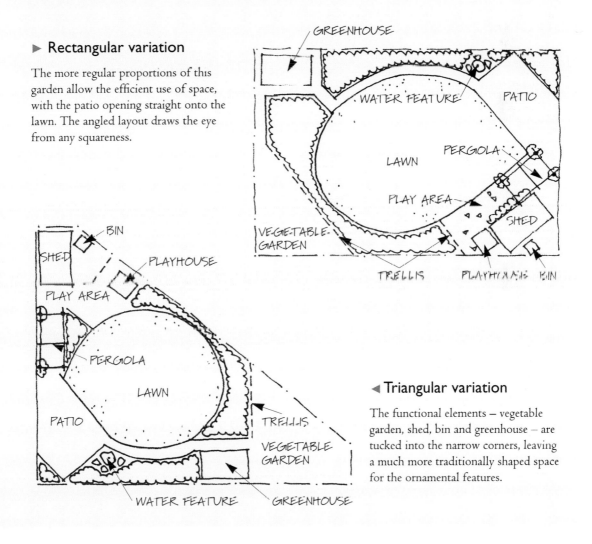

◄ Triangular variation

The functional elements — vegetable garden, shed, bin and greenhouse — are tucked into the narrow corners, leaving a much more traditionally shaped space for the ornamental features.

Colour-themed Garden

The design

At first glance, long, narrow gardens can appear to offer very few opportunities to create worthwhile designs. This is mainly because of the claustrophobic 'tunnel' effect, which is caused by the side boundaries being long and close together. However, one of the most successful ways to treat such a garden, whether it's large or small, is to divide it into two or three individual areas, each separated from the other by some form of barrier. The barrier can be solid, like a wall, or more transparent, such as a trellis screen, or it can take the form of a bed of tall planting.

In this particular example, the garden is effectively divided into three by the use of trellis panels and a pergola. Each space is linked to the one next to it by means of an arch or gateway, in this case the end bay of the pergola itself being the gateway. These devices allow just enough of a view through to suggest that the garden is actually larger but they invite further inspection to see what really lies beyond.

Because the three spaces are virtually independent, each can be treated in an entirely separate way to the others without appearing to be out of place. The patio area nearest the house has therefore been made rather formal in its layout, with limited planting and an emphasis on the use of square or rectangular shapes and straight lines. Moving further along to the centre of the garden, informal planting almost completely dominates the space and the stone path leading through it is there almost as a necessary intrusion, purely for practicality's sake. Finally, the far end of the garden is revealed beneath the canopy of the pergola as a quiet blend of informal borders and slightly more formal paving, terminating in a delicate gazebo, which faces back across a small lawn to focus on an attractive glazed urn nestling among the planting.

The contrast between these three spaces is deliberately exaggerated even more by restricting the planting within each of them to a very limited colour palette or theme – the nearer patio garden uses reds and oranges, the central, 'woodland' garden concentrates on pinks and yellows, and the distant quiet garden is restricted to blues and white. The choice of these particular combinations is quite deliberate because reds and oranges appear to be nearer than pinks and yellows, while blues suggest far distance. This property of colours is particularly valuable in any small garden since it can be used as a way of making the garden appear larger than it actually is.

Limiting your choice of flower colours to just two or three – such as the blue and pink selected here – creates a very striking effect.

The planting

Reds and oranges are very strong, vibrant colours, and using them excessively in a small, confined space could prove to be quite disturbing. A limited number of plants is therefore selected for the patio area to extend the flowering times over a long period. Additionally, one or two plants have been included purely for the neutralizing effect of their foliage and to act as a foil to the bright colours. *Artemisia* 'Powis Castle', hellebore (*Helleborus argutifolius*) and ivy (*Hedera hibernica*, syn. *H. helix* subsp. *hibernica*) are excellent for this purpose.

In the pink and yellow 'woodland' garden, plants have been selected for their size and habit as well as for their colour, so that they provide more variation and avoid making this area look too flat. Shrubs such as golden dogwood (*Cornus alba* 'Aurea') and golden privet (*Ligustrum* 'Vicaryi') give height, while perennials like yellow water flag (*Iris pseudacorus*) are used to add a degree of spikiness.

At the far end of the garden, beyond the pergola, a mix of shrubs, perennials and climbers is chosen to provide a long season of both flower and foliage interest and at the same time to mask and soften the boundary walls.

The features

Mixed sizes of rectangular York flagstones are used to create the generous patio at the back and side of the house. On the far side of the patio, a screen of wooden arched trellis panels is stained dark green to

PLANTING PLAN

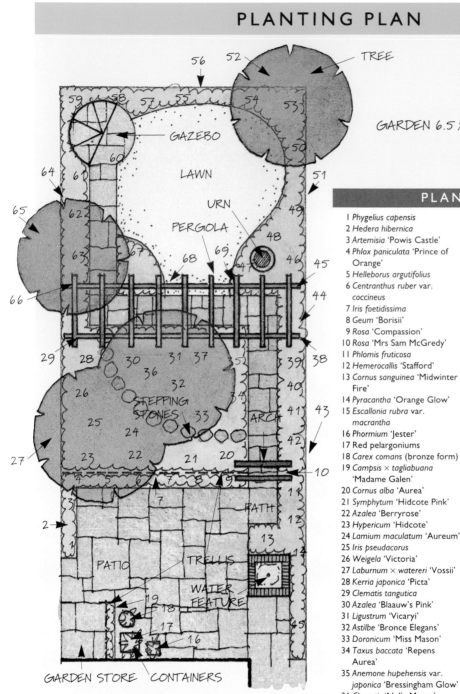

56 52 TREE

59 58 57 55 54 53

GAZEBO

GARDEN 6.5 x 15m (21 x 49ft)

LAWN

64 61 51

65 62

URN

PERGOLA 49

66 63 67 48

68 69 47 46 45

44

29 28 30 31 37 35 39 38

36 40

26 32 34

STEPPING
STONES 33 ARCH 41 43

25 24 42

27 23 22 21 20

4 5 6 7 8 9 10

3 11

7 PATH

2 12

13

14

PATIO TRELLIS

WATER
FEATURE 19 18 45

17

16

GARDEN STORE CONTAINERS

PLANT LIST

1 *Phygelius capensis*
2 *Hedera hibernica*
3 *Artemisia* 'Powis Castle'
4 *Phlox paniculata* 'Prince of Orange'
5 *Helleborus argutifolius*
6 *Centranthus ruber* var. *coccineus*
7 *Iris foetidissima*
8 *Geum* 'Borisii'
9 *Rosa* 'Compassion'
10 *Rosa* 'Mrs Sam McGredy'
11 *Phlomis fruticosa*
12 *Hemerocallis* 'Stafford'
13 *Cornus sanguinea* 'Midwinter Fire'
14 *Pyracantha* 'Orange Glow'
15 *Escallonia rubra* var. *macrantha*
16 *Phormium* 'Jester'
17 Red pelargoniums
18 *Carex comans* (bronze form)
19 *Campsis* × *tagliabuana* 'Madame Galen'
20 *Cornus alba* 'Aurea'
21 *Symphytum* 'Hidcote Pink'
22 *Azalea* 'Berryrose'
23 *Hypericum* 'Hidcote'
24 *Lamium maculatum* 'Aureum'
25 *Iris pseudacorus*
26 *Weigela* 'Victoria'
27 *Laburnum* × *watereri* 'Vossii'
28 *Kerria japonica* 'Picta'
29 *Clematis tangutica*
30 *Azalea* 'Blaauw's Pink'
31 *Ligustrum* 'Vicaryi'
32 *Astilbe* 'Bronce Elegans'
33 *Doronicum* 'Miss Mason'
34 *Taxus baccata* 'Repens Aurea'
35 *Anemone hupehensis* var. *japonica* 'Bressingham Glow'
36 *Clematis* 'Nelly Moser'
37 *Lonicera periclymenum* 'Graham Thomas'
38 *Rosa* 'Pink Perpétué'
39 *Pittosporum tenuifolium* 'Warnham Gold'
40 *Aster novi-belgii* 'Little Pink Beauty'
41 *Rosa* 'Bonica'
42 *Solidago* 'Cloth of Gold'
43 *Lonicera japonica* 'Aureoreticulata'
44 *Elaeagnus* × *ebbingei*
45 *Clematis alpina*
46 *Ceanothus* 'Delight'
47 *Leucanthemum* × *superbum* 'Snowcap'
48 *Geranium wallichianum* 'Buxton's Variety'
49 *Miscanthus* 'Silberfeder'
50 *Delphinium* Black Knight Group
51 *Clematis* 'Henryi'
52 *Prunus serrula*
53 *Hydrangea macrophylla* 'Lanarth White'
54 *Iris sibirica* 'Perry's Blue'
55 *Potentilla fruticosa* 'Abbotswood'
56 *Clematis flammula*
57 *Aconitum carmichaelii* 'Arendsii'
58 *Rosa* 'Iceberg'
59 *Ceanothus* × *delileanus* 'Gloire de Versailles'
60 *Clematis* 'The President'
61 *Hydrangea paniculata* 'Kyushu'
62 *Hibiscus syriacus* 'Oiseau Bleu'
63 *Echinacea purpurea* 'White Lustre'
64 *Hydrangea anomala* subsp. *petiolaris*
65 *Catalpa bignonioides*
66 *Clematis alpina* 'Frances Rivis'
67 *Viburnum plicatum* 'Mariesii'
68 *Jasminum officinale* f. *affine*
69 *Clematis* 'Perle d'Azur'

provide extra background colour to the red and orange flowers. Similar trellis is used in one corner of the patio to divide off a small section of paving, which can then be used as an outside storage area. On the right-hand side of the patio is a small, square raised pool, made from old bricks that match the boundary walls and lined with a flexible liner to make it watertight. A gentle fountain completes the effect. In the far right-hand corner a matching flagstone path leads into the 'woodland' garden, through a green archway that matches the style and colour of the trellis.

On the other side of this archway, the paving diverges with a stepping stone path of sawn-log rounds cutting diagonally to the left through the planting and between a 'gateway' formed by two closely planted *Laburnum × watereri* 'Vossii'. The York stone path continues straight on, before turning left across the garden beneath a rustic pergola made up of round, unpeeled larch poles. Turning right at the far side of the garden, the path then continues to the end to become a small circular plinth on which is fixed a white-painted, semicircular, wrought iron gazebo, covered by climbing roses (*Rosa* 'Iceberg') and *Clematis* 'The President' and with a small seat beneath.

As a final touch, a large, dark blue, glazed urn filled with white petunias forms a focal point when it is viewed not only from the gazebo but also from the other end of the garden, framed through the green arch and the end bay of the pergola.

VARIATIONS

▶ Wide, shallow variation

The carefully angled patio and path combine with the almost circular lawn to camouflage the difficult proportions of the garden, yet the trellis and pergola still allow it to be divided into three theme areas.

◀ Corner variation

This shape lends itself perfectly to being divided into three roughly equal spaces by the pergola and trellis without the overall angular arrangement being too obvious.

Water Garden

The design

Water, as a feature, is almost a standard requirement of any garden since it can be included in all shapes or sizes, from a tiny bubble fountain to a small lake. More often than not, however, a water feature is ancillary to the other elements in the garden and is, consequently, on a comparatively small scale. In this garden, however, water is the dominant feature, and the whole garden revolves around a substantial split-level pool arrangement.

The use of angular and circular themes is an effective way of disguising the boundaries of square gardens, and here these two devices are combined. The lower and larger of the two pools is partially defined by the edges of an L-shaped deck, which is set at an angle to the house, while the upper, smaller pool is enclosed behind by a planting area created by a semicircular path, which links each end of the deck and forms a 'walk' around the garden. This 'walk' leads to a statue in one corner of the garden and a pergola with a seat in the other. The deck arrangement creates a triangle of space, which is useful as a storage area hidden from view by a bamboo screen.

Although this garden is not intended to replicate what is often termed a 'Japanese' garden, nevertheless the choice of materials and plants lends a certain calm, Oriental feel to the whole design.

The planting

Water generally creates a mood of tranquillity and peace, and so the planting around this garden is carefully chosen to reflect this idea. The colours of the flowers are therefore softer, and the more vibrant reds and bright oranges are generally avoided in favour of using colours such as pinks and yellows – for example, a day lily (*Hemerocallis* 'Pink Damask') and *Mahonia × media* 'Charity'. Masking the corners and boundaries is vital if the exact shape and size of this garden are not to be immediately obvious, and much of the planting, including the two trees – a willow (*Salix babylonica* 'Crispa') and Italian alder (*Alnus cordata*) – is selected for that purpose.

A greater emphasis is also placed on choosing plants for their foliage, both as a foil or background to other plants, such as *Elaeagnus × ebbingei*, and as features in their own right, such as the variegated Westonbirt dogwood (*Cornus alba* 'Sibirica Variegata'). The Oriental influence is underlined by the inclusion of bamboos – anceps bamboo (*Yushania anceps*, syn. *Arundinaria anceps*, *A. jaunsarensis*) and *Pleioblastus variegatus* (syn. *Arundinaria fortunei*, *A. variegata*) – and grasses – *Miscanthus sinensis* 'Malepartus' and switch grass (*Panicum virgatum* 'Rubrum').

Aquatic plants are used in the lower pool, both to soften the somewhat severe edges of the deck and to create additional reflections in the water. They are planted in baskets of soil, which are placed on marginal shelves built just inside the edge of the pool 15–23cm (6–9in) below the water level.

In the left-hand bed behind the lower pool, a flowering dogwood (*Cornus kousa* var. *chinensis*) is carefully positioned so that it provides a dramatic reflection in the water's surface with its striking flowering bracts in spring and its autumn colour.

The features

At the centre of the garden are the split-level pools. The lower pool is constructed of concrete. The inner walls have been painted with proprietary black pond paint both to waterproof it and to increase the effect of depth. The upper pool is essentially a brick box, rendered internally with a waterproof sand–cement mortar and also painted black. The blue-grey bricks of this upper pool create dark reflections in the lower pool, adding to the depth and mystery of the water. A submersible pump in the lower pool supplies water to the upper pool via a concealed flexible pipe, and it emerges through a geyser or

The tiny fountain in this simple raised pool matches the scale and restful mood of this tiny foliage garden.

PLANTING PLAN

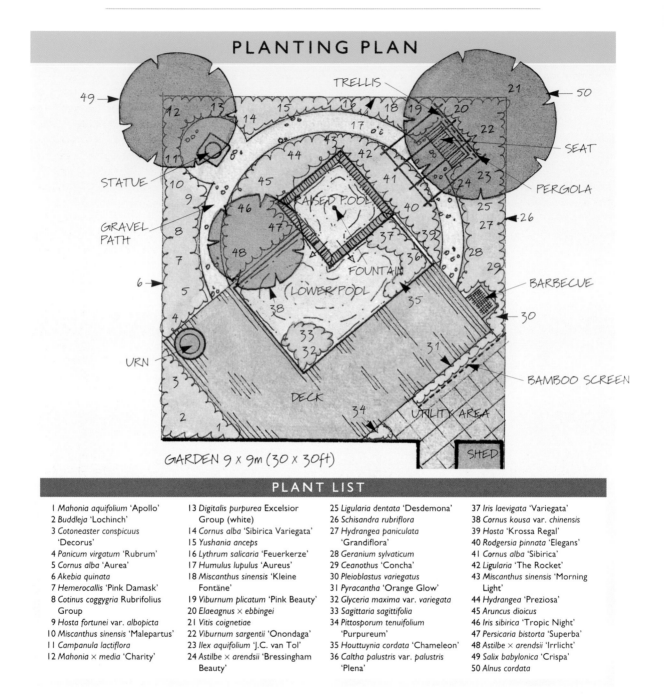

49
50
TRELLIS
21
42 13 15 16 18 19 20
14 17 22
SEAT
11 8 43 42
STATUE 10 44 41 23
9 RAISED POOL 24 PERGOLA
45 25
GRAVEL 46 40 27 26
PATH 8 47 FOUNTAIN 39 28
6 7 48 (LOWER POOL) 37 29 BARBECUE
5 38 36 30
4 35
URN 3 33 31 BAMBOO SCREEN
32
2 DECK 34
1 UTILITY AREA
SHED

GARDEN 9 x 9m (30 x 30ft)

PLANT LIST

1 *Mahonia aquifolium* 'Apollo'
2 *Buddleja* 'Lochinch'
3 *Cotoneaster conspicuus* 'Decorus'
4 *Panicum virgatum* 'Rubrum'
5 *Cornus alba* 'Aurea'
6 *Akebia quinata*
7 *Hemerocallis* 'Pink Damask'
8 *Cotinus coggygria* Rubrifolius Group
9 *Hosta fortunei* var. *albopicta*
10 *Miscanthus sinensis* 'Malepartus'
11 *Campanula lactiflora*
12 *Mahonia* × *media* 'Charity'

13 *Digitalis purpurea* Excelsior Group (white)
14 *Cornus alba* 'Sibirica Variegata'
15 *Yushania anceps*
16 *Lythrum salicaria* 'Feuerkerze'
17 *Humulus lupulus* 'Aureus'
18 *Miscanthus sinensis* 'Kleine Fontäne'
19 *Viburnum plicatum* 'Pink Beauty'
20 *Elaeagnus* × *ebbingei*
21 *Vitis coignetiae*
22 *Viburnum sargentii* 'Onondaga'
23 *Ilex aquifolium* 'J.C. van Tol'
24 *Astilbe* × *arendsii* 'Bressingham Beauty'

25 *Ligularia dentata* 'Desdemona'
26 *Schisandra rubriflora*
27 *Hydrangea paniculata* 'Grandiflora'
28 *Geranium sylvaticum*
29 *Ceanothus* 'Concha'
30 *Pleioblastus variegatus*
31 *Pyracantha* 'Orange Glow'
32 *Glyceria maxima* var. *variegata*
33 *Sagittaria sagittifolia*
34 *Pittosporum tenuifolium* 'Purpureum'
35 *Houttuynia cordata* 'Chameleon'
36 *Caltha palustris* var. *palustris* 'Plena'

37 *Iris laevigata* 'Variegata'
38 *Cornus kousa* var. *chinensis*
39 *Hosta* 'Krossa Regal'
40 *Rodgersia pinnata* 'Elegans'
41 *Cornus alba* 'Sibirica'
42 *Ligularia* 'The Rocket'
43 *Miscanthus sinensis* 'Morning Light'
44 *Hydrangea* 'Preziosa'
45 *Aruncus dioicus*
46 *Iris sibirica* 'Tropic Night'
47 *Persicaria bistorta* 'Superba'
48 *Astilbe* × *arendsii* 'Irrlicht'
49 *Salix babylonica* 'Crispa'
50 *Alnus cordata*

'bubble' fountain before returning to the lower level again over two cascades made of thin, dark slate.

Forming two sides of the larger pool, the deck is made from thin planks of durable sustainable hardwood. An alternative would be pressure-treated softwood, which is more economical. Whatever wood is chosen, it is left unstained to weather to a natural finish. The planks are nailed to joists in the same way as a wooden floor, and these, in turn, are supported by low concrete or brick piers.

In the far right-hand corner is a pergola, built from round steel tubes, about 7.5cm (3in) in diameter, which are painted blue-grey to complement the brick used in the pool. Between the two rear posts of the pergola, a diamond trellis panel made of thin steel bars, 10–12mm (½in) in diameter, is fixed; this, too, is painted blue-grey. Crimson glory vine (*Vitis coignetiae*) is trained up this panel, and it will ultimately grow up and over the pergola and form a canopy above a simple seat on the gravel beneath.

The pergola is reached by a narrow, timber-edged gravel path leading from the deck. This path continues around the garden in a circular fashion, and in the far left-hand corner it widens to form a small semicircle on which an Oriental statuette is placed, beneath the willow. The path then narrows again, before rejoining the deck at the other side.

The utility area is hidden from view by a screen made from thick bamboo canes, which are fixed vertically to two or three horizontal wooden rails screwed or nailed to vertical posts at each end. At the far right hand end of the deck is a small space set aside for a barbecue or another statue. Completing the design is a large Cretan urn, which sits on one corner of the deck set against the delicate stems and seedheads of the switch grass immediately behind it.

VARIATIONS

▶ Long, narrow variation

The angle of the pools and deck is changed to mirror that of the corner-to-corner diagonal. Having the path on one side only of the garden makes space for extra planting in front of the pergola for greater privacy and interest.

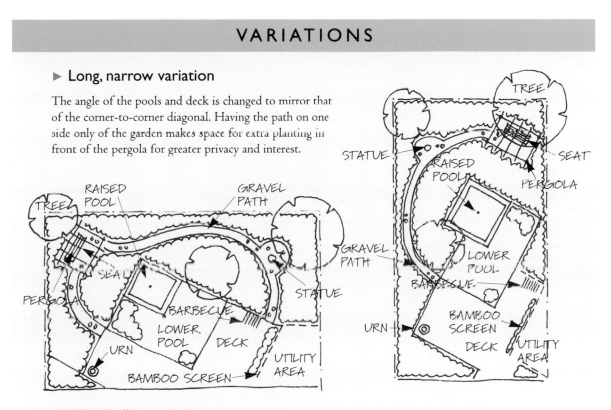

▲ Wide, shallow variation

The diagonal axis is used to draw attention away from the shallowness of this garden, and this is helped by the curving paths and corner focal points created by the pergola and statue.

Year-round Garden

The design

The appeal of a garden that is attractive throughout the year is obvious, and in larger gardens there is generally enough space for an extensive range of plant varieties to provide interest at almost any time. Smaller gardens, however, have far less available space, and the selection of plants to maintain a similar level of interest becomes much more critical. The overall garden design itself is no less important, because it must not only create an acceptable visual whole but also make the most efficient use of the space, leaving the maximum room possible for plants.

The design of this particular small, triangular garden successfully incorporates a range of features and quite generous planting in a cohesive way that is both practical and attractive. Disguising the odd shape of the plot is achieved principally by turning the patio through 45 degrees and making the perimeter border curved and informal. The combination of taller shrubs and climbers softens and hides the boundary fence, while the use of three small trees adds an extra vertical dimension to the garden as well as giving some extra privacy and screening.

In the foreground of the patio, a simple water feature acts as a focal point, and this is counterbalanced by an octagonal summerhouse in the far corner, neatly tucked into the planting. A simple arch acts as a divider between the ornamental patio area and the more functional utility area, which is located towards the side of the house.

Beyond the arch, a strongly curving brick path separates the water feature from a gravel area and leads to a small greenhouse. The gravel area can be used for standing out pot-grown herbs and other container-grown plants.

The planting

The effectiveness of the planting in this garden relies just as much on foliage, stems and fruit as it does on flowers, and every variety is carefully chosen to provide one or more of these features. Each of the three trees has its own appeal – the yellow fruits of the crab apple *Malus* × *zumi* 'Golden Hornet' in the autumn, the delicate spring flowers of the ornamental cherry *Prunus* 'Chôshû-hizakura' (syn. *P.* 'Hisakura'), and the brilliant white winter bark of the birch *Betula utilis* var. *jacquemontii*. Critical to almost any planting scheme are evergreens, which are often used purely as green foils to set off other, choicer plants. Here, however, they are selected for their own interest, either as climbers, such as ivy (*Hedera helix* 'Glacier'), or as shrubs, such as the moonlight holly (*Ilex aquifolium* 'Flavescens'). Contrast to the more rounded habit of some of the shrubs and perennials is provided by spiky-leaved or upright plants – fishpole bamboo (*Phyllostachys aurea*) and montbretia (*Crocosmia* 'Bressingham Beacon'), for example. Plants that provide both flower and scent are especially valuable, and in particular *Viburnum farreri*, which has strongly perfumed white flowers in late winter.

Temporary splashes of colour are provided by pots of summer annuals, spring bulbs and winter bedding according to the season, and these are placed on the gravel area among pots of herbs, such as parsley, sage, chives and marjoram, and on the patio.

Bulbs are also used in the perimeter border to provide additional interest, particularly early-flowering dwarf varieties such as crocus, snowdrop (*Galanthus* spp.) and winter aconite (*Eranthis hyemalis*), all of which can flower, grow and die down again before the larger shrubs and perennials leaf out.

The features

The patio immediately outside the french windows is made of square, buff-coloured imitation stone slabs, laid at 45 degrees to the house. This paving continues to the left of the patio to form a small outdoor storage area down the side of the house, which is secured by means of a trellis gate, stained

Perennials are essential in a year-round garden for their wonderful range of colours and flowering times.

grey. At the other end of the patio, the same style of paving carries on beneath the simple arch to form a hard-standing between the end of an aluminium greenhouse and a small salad garden on the right-hand side of the house. This hardstanding is positioned well away from the general views of the garden and offers an ideal place for drying clothes and so on.

A path of dark brown paving bricks connects the stone-effect paving to the far end of the greenhouse and at the same time separates the utility part of the garden from the ornamental section. The bricks are laid stretcher bond – that is, end to end – and the pattern that is created emphasizes the bold curve of the path.

Making an intriguing foreground feature in the triangle between the patio and the brick path is a small fountain, which emerges through a layer of

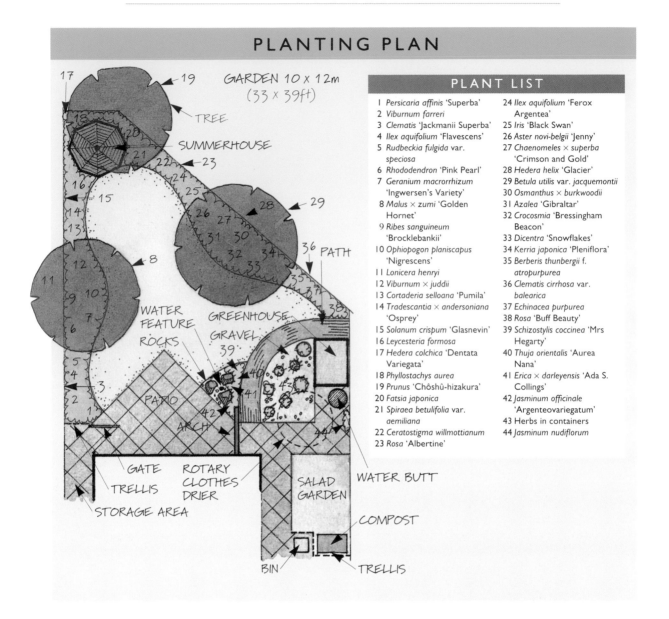

PLANTING PLAN

GARDEN 10 x 12m
(33 x 39ft)

17 · 19 · TREE · SUMMERHOUSE · 18 · 20 · 21 · 22 · 23 · 16 · 24 · 15 · 25 · 14 · 13 · 26 · 27 · 31 · 30 · 28 · 29 · 12 · 32 · 34 · 33 · 36 PATH · 8 · 35 · 11 · 9 10 · 37 · 7 · 38 · 6 · WATER FEATURE · GREENHOUSE · 5 · ROCKS · GRAVEL · 4 · 39 · 3 · 40 · 2 · 41 · 42 · PATIO · 43 · 1 · ARCH · 44 · GATE · ROTARY CLOTHES DRIER · SALAD GARDEN · WATER BUTT · TRELLIS · STORAGE AREA · COMPOST · BIN · TRELLIS

PLANT LIST

1 *Persicaria affinis* 'Superba'
2 *Viburnum farreri*
3 *Clematis* 'Jackmanii Superba'
4 *Ilex aquifolium* 'Flavescens'
5 *Rudbeckia fulgida* var. *speciosa*
6 *Rhododendron* 'Pink Pearl'
7 *Geranium macrorrhizum* 'Ingwersen's Variety'
8 *Malus × zumi* 'Golden Hornet'
9 *Ribes sanguineum* 'Brocklebankii'
10 *Ophiopogon planiscapus* 'Nigrescens'
11 *Lonicera henryi*
12 *Viburnum × juddii*
13 *Cortaderia selloana* 'Pumila'
14 *Tradescantia × andersoniana* 'Osprey'
15 *Solanum crispum* 'Glasnevin'
16 *Leycesteria formosa*
17 *Hedera colchica* 'Dentata Variegata'
18 *Phyllostachys aurea*
19 *Prunus* 'Chôshû-hizakura'
20 *Fatsia japonica*
21 *Spiraea betulifolia* var. *aemiliana*
22 *Ceratostigma willmottianum*
23 *Rosa* 'Albertine'

24 *Ilex aquifolium* 'Ferox Argentea'
25 *Iris* 'Black Swan'
26 *Aster novi-belgii* 'Jenny'
27 *Chaenomeles × superba* 'Crimson and Gold'
28 *Hedera helix* 'Glacier'
29 *Betula utilis* var. *jacquemontii*
30 *Osmanthus × burkwoodii*
31 *Azalea* 'Gibraltar'
32 *Crocosmia* 'Bressingham Beacon'
33 *Dicentra* 'Snowflakes'
34 *Kerria japonica* 'Pleniflora'
35 *Berberis thunbergii* f. *atropurpurea*
36 *Clematis cirrhosa* var. *balearica*
37 *Echinacea purpurea*
38 *Rosa* 'Buff Beauty'
39 *Schizostylis coccinea* 'Mrs Hegarty'
40 *Thuja orientalis* 'Aurea Nana'
41 *Erica × darleyensis* 'Ada S. Collings'
42 *Jasminum officinale* 'Argenteovariegatum'
43 Herbs in containers
44 *Jasminum nudiflorum*

rocks, cobbles and pebbles suspended on steel mesh laid above a tank or sump let into the ground below. It is ideally placed to catch sunlight on a hot day and provides a soothing, cooling effect.

The wooden arch is made from sawn softwood. It is stained black and acts as support for a variegated jasmine (*Jasminum officinale* 'Argenteovariegatum'), which stands out dramatically against the dark timber and provides a delicious fragrance, which will drift onto the nearby patio and through the kitchen window.

The space enclosed by the brick path, greenhouse and paved utility area is mulched with pale stone chippings to match the colour of the flagstones. This creates an ideal, sunny and sheltered environment on which to place tubs and containers of herbs, annuals or even permanent plantings, such as hosta and skimmia. Ideally, the gravel needs to be laid on top of a proprietary porous mulching membrane or a sheet of perforated heavy duty black polythene. This will not only prevent any subsequent weed growth pushing up through the gravel, but will also avoid the gravel itself being trodden down and mixed into the soil beneath.

At the side of the house near the back door there is space for a small salad or vegetable garden. Clearly, this is not large enough to grow vast amounts of crops, but it is ideal for trying out unusual varieties, such as kohl-rabi or celeriac, or those that are best appreciated when picked young and absolutely fresh, like lettuce, spinach and radishes.

At the far end of the garden is an octagonal cedarwood summerhouse with a cedar shingle roof, creating a striking focal point seen from the house and patio. It is framed by the planting behind and around.

The whole garden is enclosed by panels of woven fencing, which are mounted between square, softwood posts treated with preservative to prevent rot. Both the panels and posts are stained mid-grey to match the trellis and gate by the outside storage area and to act as an effective backcloth to the perimeter planting.

VARIATIONS

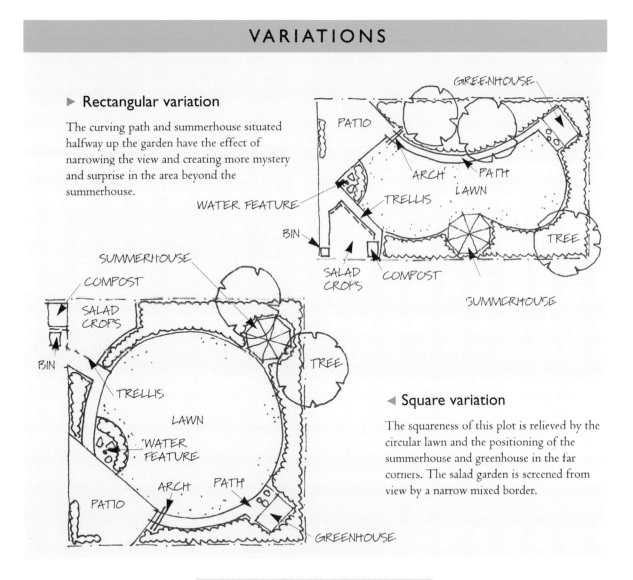

► **Rectangular variation**

The curving path and summerhouse situated halfway up the garden have the effect of narrowing the view and creating more mystery and surprise in the area beyond the summerhouse.

◄ **Square variation**

The squareness of this plot is relieved by the circular lawn and the positioning of the summerhouse and greenhouse in the far corners. The salad garden is screened from view by a narrow mixed border.

Scented Garden

The design

Scent is one aspect of gardens that is often overlooked, yet it can make as important a contribution to the overall effect as the most flamboyant flower or exotically patterned leaf.

While some plant scents are heavy, almost to the point of being overpowering or sickly, others are quite delicate and have a fragrance that can be detected only in its very immediate surroundings. Not all scent is from flowers, and there are many plants whose chief attraction derives from the pleasant aroma of their foliage – some will freely exude it, while others are reluctant to do so until the leaves are crushed or rubbed by inquiring fingers.

Any style of garden can contain perfumed planting, but in this example of a corner plot the emphasis is on informality and practicality. The design itself is inherently simple, with the arc of the patio edge leading onto a gently curving lawn, which links both ends of the garden and at the same time creates some quite generous areas of planting to hide the square corners of the plot.

At the rear of the patio, screened from view, is a paved area that is used to accommodate the more basic features, including a shed, which is further hidden by shrub planting and a tree. In the diagonally opposite corner another tree provides balance and has a small sitting area beneath it from which to look back over the garden.

In this garden scent is not confined to the flowers, like the roses (*Rosa* 'Aloha' and *R.* 'Fritz Nobis'), but is also found in foliage of *Artemisia* and variegated apple mint.

A second axis is developed by placing a simple pool in the remaining corner of the garden across from the patio, to which it is linked by a stepping-stone path, which passes through a small bed near the corner of the house and across the lawn.

A path continues from the patio and down the side of the house to the front gate, passing as it does so beneath a series of arches covered in climbers. A matching arch at the back of the patio creates an entrance to the shed and utility area.

The planting

It would be a relatively simple matter to fill a small garden with a collection of plants to provide scent at various times of the year with their perfumed flowers and aromatic foliage. However, what the garden might look like as a composition could be anybody's guess. In this corner garden plants are therefore selected not only for their fragrant qualities at different times of the year but also for their other attributes of flower, foliage and shape, and they are put together in a way that creates an effective overall composition and provides some interest at all times. Some of the plants are attractive all year round – the firethorn (*Pyracantha* 'Orange Glow'), for example, which has evergreen foliage, gently scented flowers and bright orange autumn berries. Others are more seasonal and will come into their own for a limited part of the year, albeit more dramatically. *Rosa* 'Graham Thomas' is a good example of such a plant – it is nothing more than bare stems from late autumn to early spring but makes up for this failing later on with glossy summer foliage and large, gorgeously scented flowers.

Having too many heavily scented plants, such as summer jasmine (*Jasminum officinale* f. *affine*), producing their perfume at the same time in a confined space might be overpowering. Here, however, the planting mixes together varieties that not only produce their scent at varying times but also in differing degrees. Richly perfumed honeysuckle (*Lonicera periclymenum* 'Serotina') with its bonus of sticky, red berries can be found alongside

PLANTING PLAN

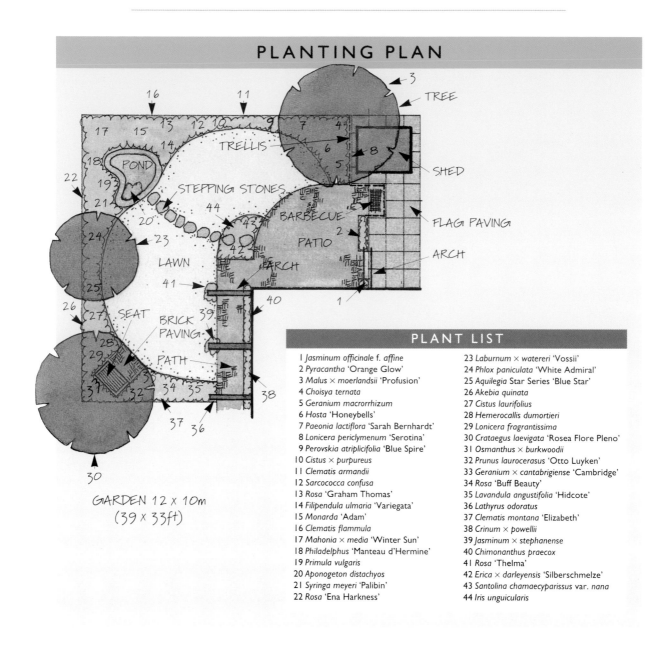

16   11   3 TREE

17 15 13 12 10   9   4
              14   TRELLIS   6   7
18 POND   19
22   21   STEPPING STONES   8   SHED
              44
24   20   23   43   BARBECUE   5   FLAG PAVING
              42   PATIO   2   ARCH
25   LAWN   41   ARCH   1
26 27 SEAT   39
28   BRICK PAVING   40
29   PATH
31 32 34 35   38
37 36
30

GARDEN 12 x 10m
(39 x 33ft)

PLANT LIST

1 *Jasminum officinale* f. *affine*	23 *Laburnum* × *watereri* 'Vossii'
2 *Pyracantha* 'Orange Glow'	24 *Phlox paniculata* 'White Admiral'
3 *Malus* × *moerlandsii* 'Profusion'	25 *Aquilegia* Star Series 'Blue Star'
4 *Choisya ternata*	26 *Akebia quinata*
5 *Geranium macrorrhizum*	27 *Cistus laurifolius*
6 *Hosta* 'Honeybells'	28 *Hemerocallis dumortieri*
7 *Paeonia lactiflora* 'Sarah Bernhardt'	29 *Lonicera fragrantissima*
8 *Lonicera periclymenum* 'Serotina'	30 *Crataegus laevigata* 'Rosea Flore Pleno'
9 *Perovskia atriplicifolia* 'Blue Spire'	31 *Osmanthus* × *burkwoodii*
10 *Cistus* × *purpureus*	32 *Prunus laurocerasus* 'Otto Luyken'
11 *Clematis armandii*	33 *Geranium* × *cantabrigiense* 'Cambridge'
12 *Sarcococca confusa*	34 *Rosa* 'Buff Beauty'
13 *Rosa* 'Graham Thomas'	35 *Lavandula angustifolia* 'Hidcote'
14 *Filipendula ulmaria* 'Variegata'	36 *Lathyrus odoratus*
15 *Monarda* 'Adam'	37 *Clematis montana* 'Elizabeth'
16 *Clematis flammula*	38 *Crinum* × *powellii*
17 *Mahonia* × *media* 'Winter Sun'	39 *Jasminum* × *stephanense*
18 *Philadelphus* 'Manteau d'Hermine'	40 *Chimonanthus praecox*
19 *Primula vulgaris*	41 *Rosa* 'Thelma'
20 *Aponogeton distachyos*	42 *Erica* × *darleyensis* 'Silberschmelze'
21 *Syringa meyeri* 'Palibin'	43 *Santolina chamaecyparissus* var. *nana*
22 *Rosa* 'Ena Harkness'	44 *Iris unguicularis*

Russian sage (*Perovskia atriplicifolia* 'Blue Spire') with its more pungent, herbal aroma. Even in the depths of winter there will be flowers and scent in this garden, provided by *Mahonia* × *media* 'Winter Sun', shrubby honeysuckle (*Lonicera fragrantissima*) and the shade-tolerant Christmas box (*Sarcococca confusa*), with its crop of black berries to follow in the summer.

The features

An old terracotta brick is used for the patio, the path down the side of the house and the tiny sitting area beneath the pink hawthorn tree (*Crataegus laevigata* 'Rosea Flore Pleno'). Laid on sand in a basketweave pattern, the brick paving enhances the slightly old-fashioned feel of the garden.

Providing a link from the patio to the pool, the stepping stone path consists of randomly shaped pieces of York stone, let into the lawn, and this blends in well both with the planting scheme and the other 'hard' materials in the garden. Smaller pieces of the same stone are laid on a bed of sand–cement mortar to form the edge of the informal pool, which is made from a flexible pond liner, and in which a water hawthorn (*Aponogeton distachyos*) creates a carpet of leaves with delicately scented flowers held above them.

The arches over the path and also at the entrance to the utility area are made from broad, thin-sectioned timbers painted white, fixed on edge at the top of matching white steel tube. The use of white makes the arches appear very light and sets off the climbers well.

In contrast, the diamond-effect wooden trellis forming the screen to the utility area and shed is stained dark brown to tone down its appearance and to allow both the plants in front of it and those growing up it to stand out more effectively. This screen is neatly dog-legged halfway along to form a small recess, which is just large enough to slot in a small barbecue.

VARIATIONS

▶ Long, narrow variation

The pond is placed halfway up the garden and the path swings strongly from left to right in front of it to disguise the irregular proportions of the space. Placing the arches over the stepping stones provides extra screening of the far end.

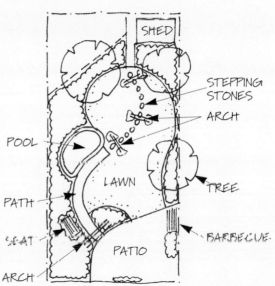

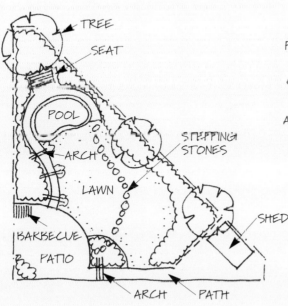

◀ Triangular variation

The path runs up to and behind the pool, which is placed in front of the far corner, before returning across the lawn to the patio. Combined with the strongly curving border, this completely disguises the straight boundaries of the garden.

Foliage Garden

The design

While there will always be a place in gardens for plants whose main attraction is their flowers, varieties with insignificant flowering attributes can tend to be neglected even though they may possess other striking qualities in the colour, shape or size of their foliage. They are more likely to be used either as a foil or backdrop to their more flamboyant flowering relations or for more mundane purposes, such as screening a compost heap.

However, a garden that consists of plants selected primarily for their foliage qualities and in which flowers are of secondary importance can be just as dramatic – if not more so – as what might be termed a conventional garden, with its preponderance of flowers at different times of the year.

To disguise the odd proportions of this wide, shallow garden, a dramatically curved paved area and lawn form a central theme, and these are backed by a generous perimeter border. The principal patio area by the house narrows to become a path, which

sweeps around the right-hand side of the garden before opening out again into a semicircular second patio area in front of a hexagonal gazebo. From here the lawn edge continues to swing around the garden, effectively cutting off the far left-hand corner and creating as it does so a useful outdoor storage area. Screened by a trellis fence, this storage area is also hidden from further view by a tree placed in the corner of the perimeter border. In the diagonally opposite corner to the tree is a small, round pool, and these two features form an axis that helps to draw attention away from the longest boundary fence. The left-hand side of the garden is basically a utility area. It is separated from the more ornamental area by a combination of arches and trellis and allows access to the front of the house.

The planting

Concealing boundaries with suitable plants is an excellent way to hide the shape and therefore the size of any garden, which always adds a degree of mystery and surprise. Climbers, particularly bold, vigorous examples, such as golden hop (*Humulus lupulus* 'Aureus'), and taller shrubs, such as *Elaeagnus* × *ebbingei* 'Limelight', are excellent for this purpose and provide a solid framework that is essential in any garden.

Variations in colour are as important as they would be with flowers, and silver- or grey-leaved subjects, such as *Artemisia* 'Powis Castle' and *Pulmonaria saccharata* Argentea Group, are particularly effective in linking together the golds, purples, reds and greens of the other plants.

In some cases, it is the habit or form of the plant that provides the real drama or effect, particularly upright or fastigiate forms. Arrow bamboo (*Pseudosasa japonica*, syn. *Arundinaria japonica*) and some of the taller grasses, such as *Miscanthus sinensis* var. *purpurascens*, are ideal examples of this.

Plain green foliage can be equally dramatic when the leaf is very large or has an unusual shape. Here *Mahonia lomariifolia* forms a majestic isolated specimen against the trellis fence.

Evergreens are essential to provide some interest in winter, and coloured or variegated forms of these make particularly good features, such as the *Pittosporum tenuifolium* 'Silver Queen' at the corner of the patio.

Smaller plants are used throughout the garden to provide infill, ground cover and edgings, with *Geranium renardii*, *Iris foetidissima* var. *citrina* and *Juniperus* × *pfitzeriana* 'Gold Sovereign' being typical of the diversity suggested in this respect.

Apart from its visual quality, one of the great bonuses of this foliage garden is that the emphasis on leaves will mean there is less bare soil available in which weed seeds can germinate – use lots of foliage for a low-maintenance garden.

The enormous variety of foliage colours and shapes available makes the use of flowers almost incidental, as in this shady border.

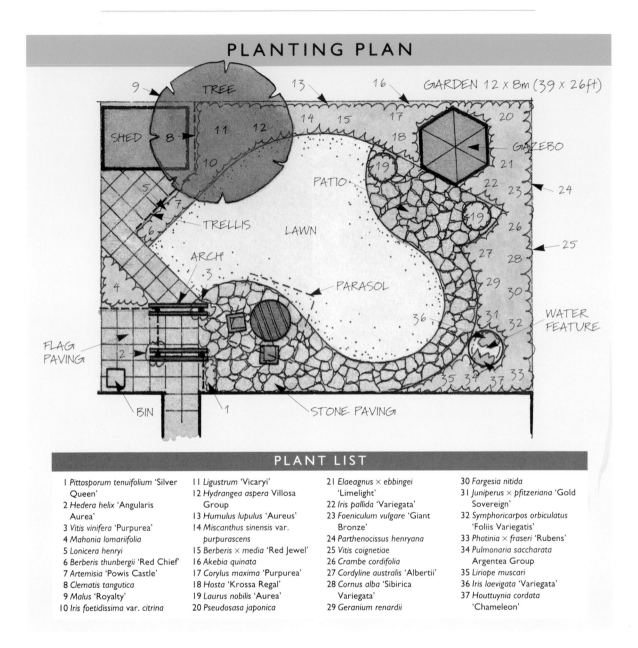

PLANTING PLAN

GARDEN 12 x 8m (39 x 26ft)

TREE · SHED · GAZEBO · PATIO · LAWN · TRELLIS · ARCH · PARASOL · WATER FEATURE · FLAG PAVING · BIN · STONE PAVING

PLANT LIST

1 *Pittosporum tenuifolium* 'Silver Queen'
2 *Hedera helix* 'Angularis Aurea'
3 *Vitis vinifera* 'Purpurea'
4 *Mahonia lomariifolia*
5 *Lonicera henryi*
6 *Berberis thunbergii* 'Red Chief'
7 *Artemisia* 'Powis Castle'
8 *Clematis tangutica*
9 *Malus* 'Royalty'
10 *Iris foetidissima* var. *citrina*

11 *Ligustrum* 'Vicaryi'
12 *Hydrangea aspera* Villosa Group
13 *Humulus lupulus* 'Aureus'
14 *Miscanthus sinensis* var. *purpurascens*
15 *Berberis* × *media* 'Red Jewel'
16 *Akebia quinata*
17 *Corylus maxima* 'Purpurea'
18 *Hosta* 'Krossa Regal'
19 *Laurus nobilis* 'Aurea'
20 *Pseudosasa japonica*

21 *Elaeagnus* × *ebbingei* 'Limelight'
22 *Iris pallida* 'Variegata'
23 *Foeniculum vulgare* 'Giant Bronze'
24 *Parthenocissus henryana*
25 *Vitis coignetiae*
26 *Crambe cordifolia*
27 *Cordyline australis* 'Albertii'
28 *Cornus alba* 'Sibirica Variegata'
29 *Geranium renardii*

30 *Fargesia nitida*
31 *Juniperus* × *pfitzeriana* 'Gold Sovereign'
32 *Symphoricarpos orbiculatus* 'Foliis Variegatis'
33 *Photinia* × *fraseri* 'Rubens'
34 *Pulmonaria saccharata* Argentea Group
35 *Liriope muscari*
36 *Iris laevigata* 'Variegata'
37 *Houttuynia cordata* 'Chameleon'

The features

Outside the french windows, the patio consists of random pieces of Cotswold or other pale-coloured stone laid in a crazy paving style with the joints pointed with a sand–cement mortar. This crazy paving is continued as a path around to the right-hand corner of the garden to form the semicircular patio behind which there is a hexagonal gazebo. The white, pre-formed walls of this gazebo are in contrast to the tall, elegant roof, which is made of fibreglass, pigmented to appear like old copper with a layer of verdigris. On either side of this crazy paving patio are topiary examples of the golden bay laurel (*Laurus nobilis* 'Aurea') planted in dark blue, heavily glazed pots.

44

A tiny, circular pre-formed pool is made out of dark blue fibreglass and contains a small fountain and marginal aquatic plants, such as *Houttuynia cordata* 'Chameleon' and *Iris laevigata* 'Variegata'. It is tucked into the border planting just off the path in front of the house.

The trellis screen that separates the ornamental and utility sections of the garden consists of arched panels made from thin steel rods, painted white, arranged and fixed in a diamond mesh pattern. Tubular steel posts are used to support not only these panels but also the arches, which are identical in outline to the trellis panels but without the diamond infill mesh.

On the patio near the house the teak garden furniture is shaded by a large, pale terracotta-coloured parasol, fluted to reflect the form of the gazebo roof in the opposite corner.

Around the garden, the boundary wall consists of smooth, whitewashed concrete blocks set between red brick piers, to set off the plants until such time as they grow large enough to hide it from view.

VARIATIONS

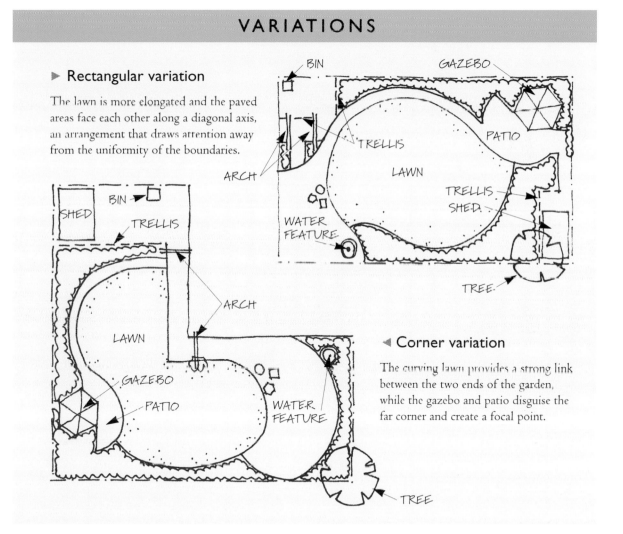

▶ **Rectangular variation**

The lawn is more elongated and the paved areas face each other along a diagonal axis, an arrangement that draws attention away from the uniformity of the boundaries.

◀ **Corner variation**

The curving lawn provides a strong link between the two ends of the garden, while the gazebo and patio disguise the far corner and create a focal point.

Courtyard Garden

The design

In practical terms a courtyard differs from a purely walled garden in that it is more likely to be partly or entirely enclosed by buildings. How the garden is used will depend partly on what the access to it is like and partly on the nature of the buildings around it.

This particular courtyard is enclosed by low buildings, which have a limited view into the courtyard itself, and so there is an element of privacy that can be used to make it into a quiet oasis away from the outside world. Being square, the space has a natural sense of formality and this idea is exploited by developing a strong, circular theme within the square, based around a central raised pool. This shape is echoed in one corner by a circular patio and in the other by a circular gazebo, and these are linked by a narrow brick path running in a circle around the entire garden. The central focal point is a fountain within the pool, and vertical interest is provided by arches over the path on either side of the gazebo.

Planting is largely confined to the area outside the path – the only exception being climbers growing up the arches and three large terracotta pots planted with cabbage trees (*Cordyline australis*) placed on the gravel near the pool.

The formality of the garden is emphasized to a degree by the mirror image that is created on each side of the diagonal axis from the gazebo in one corner to the patio in the other. An urn and statue, set among the perimeter planting in the other two corners, act as lesser focal points.

The planting

Enclosing a garden with brick or stone walls is a good way to create a sheltered and protected environment for plants, and a smaller space is likely to be even more so. The planting design for this courtyard garden takes advantage of this fact by incorporating a number of plants that might not thrive if they were planted in a more open, unprotected situation.

Phlomis chrysophylla, French lavender (*Lavandula stoechas* 'Helmsdale') and *Melianthus major* are all plants that will grow well in this garden. Walls that catch the sun are likely to be even more hospitable, and so climbers and wall shrubs, such as the slightly tender primrose jasmine (*Jasminum mesnyi*, syn. *J. primulinum*) and the exotic-looking trumpet vine (*Campsis radicans*), can be used to provide dramatic flower colour.

Structure is given to the planting, particularly in the corners where the border is more generous, by the use of larger shrubs and bamboos, including *Pittosporum tobira*, *Azara serrata*, *Bambusa gracillima* and *Phyllostachys aureosulcata* 'Aureocaulis'.

Low planting of grasses, such as blue fescue (*Festuca glauca* 'Blauglut'), and of perennials, such as lady's mantle (*Alchemilla mollis*), is used to soften the outer edge of the brick path. Climbers are used widely to take advantage of the surrounding walls, the arches and the gazebo, with roses being particularly featured.

The features

At the heart of the design is the raised circular pool, which is made from terracotta-coloured brick and lined with a flexible liner. In the centre of this is a white marble fountain, which creates a dramatic

Cream walls lighten this space and are an excellent foil for plants and features like the ornate trellis and fountain.

PLANTING PLAN

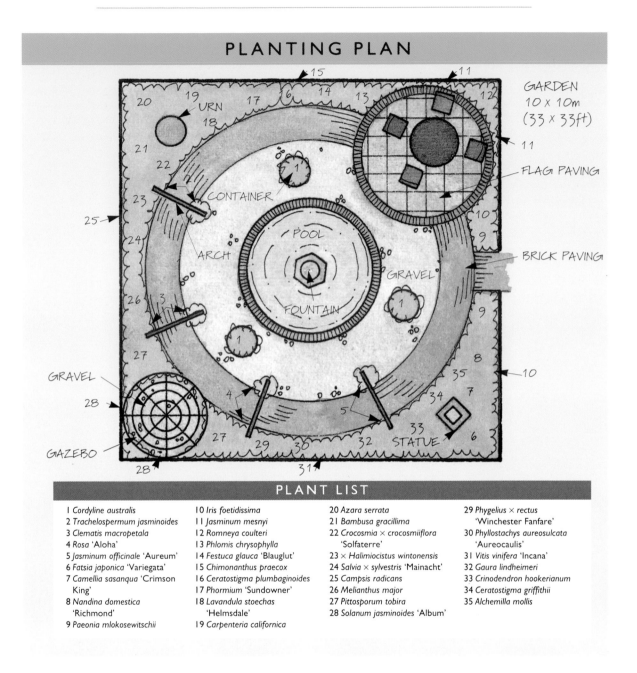

GARDEN
10 x 10m
(33 x 33ft)

URN

CONTAINER

POOL

ARCH

FOUNTAIN

GRAVEL

FLAG PAVING

BRICK PAVING

GRAVEL

STATUE

GAZEBO

PLANT LIST

1 *Cordyline australis*	10 *Iris foetidissima*	20 *Azara serrata*	29 *Phygelius × rectus*
2 *Trachelospermum jasminoides*	11 *Jasminum mesnyi*	21 *Bambusa gracillima*	'Winchester Fanfare'
3 *Clematis macropetala*	12 *Romneya coulteri*	22 *Crocosmia × crocosmiiflora*	30 *Phyllostachys aureosulcata*
4 *Rosa* 'Aloha'	13 *Phlomis chrysophylla*	'Solfaterre'	'Aureocaulis'
5 *Jasminum officinale* 'Aureum'	14 *Festuca glauca* 'Blauglut'	23 *× Halimiocistus wintonensis*	31 *Vitis vinifera* 'Incana'
6 *Fatsia japonica* 'Variegata'	15 *Chimonanthus praecox*	24 *Salvia × sylvestris* 'Mainacht'	32 *Gaura lindheimeri*
7 *Camellia sasanqua* 'Crimson	16 *Ceratostigma plumbaginoides*	25 *Campsis radicans*	33 *Crinodendron hookerianum*
King'	17 *Phormium* 'Sundowner'	26 *Melianthus major*	34 *Ceratostigma griffithii*
8 *Nandina domestica*	18 *Lavandula stoechas*	27 *Pittosporum tobira*	35 *Alchemilla mollis*
'Richmond'	'Helmsdale'	28 *Solanum jasminoides* 'Album'	
9 *Paeonia mlokosewitschii*	19 *Carpenteria californica*		

column of water via a submersible pump in the pool.

Around the pool is a circular path, built from the same brick as the wall of the pool, and laid stretcher bond (end to end) to emphasize the concentric circles of the layout. The space between these two features is covered in white stone chippings, which contrast

strikingly with the red brick and also reflect light back up on to the enclosing buildings. The circular patio, which is picked out in the same brick, uses square concrete flagstones finished in white exposed aggregate to echo the colour of the chippings.

In the opposite corner a smaller brick circle is infilled with the same white chippings and forms the base for a white, wrought iron gazebo covered in potato vine (*Solanum jasminoides* 'Album'). The abundance of white flowers and white materials provides a dramatic highlight and theme in this particular corner, but by way of stark contrast, the simple semicircular bench inside the gazebo is painted jet black.

The four arches spanning the path are made from heavy, square-sectioned oak posts, which are left to weather naturally to a beautiful silver-grey. Between the tops of the posts hang swags made from thick natural rope, and these provide a softer, more sympathetic feel than stiff wooden or metal cross-rails might.

The lesser focal points – the urn and statue – lie in diagonally opposite corners, with their bases softened by the low planting around them. In keeping with the earlier theme, the simple, traditionally shaped urn is glazed white. The statue or sculpture, on the other hand, is made from chromium-plated steel to provide another element of surprise and contrast.

As a final touch, the surrounding walls are painted white to give the whole garden more light and to generate a more spacious and airy feel to the courtyard.

VARIATIONS

▶ Long, narrow variation

The three circular elements – gazebo, pool and flag paving – are staggered, with the main path meandering across to one side and back again, drawing the eye away from the long, straight boundaries.

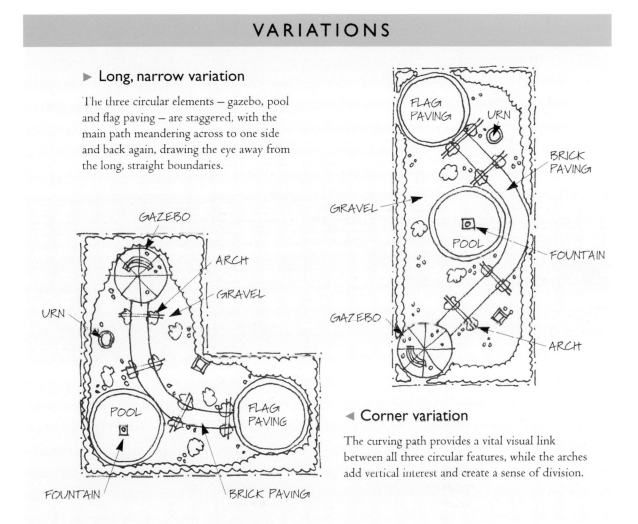

◀ Corner variation

The curving path provides a vital visual link between all three circular features, while the arches add vertical interest and create a sense of division.

Formal Garden

The design

This design is an excellent example of how the principles of formality – using symmetry, strong geometric shapes and patterns and restrained planting – can be applied even to the smallest of gardens. Normally, where informality is required, it is desirable or even necessary to disguise or hide any straight boundaries and corners. However, in a situation such as this, the square or rectangular shape of a plot can actually be used to advantage in order to maximize the formal character.

In this example, the longest dimension of the garden is emphasized by creating an axis running

from end to end down the centre to increase the feeling of depth. The right-hand side of the garden then becomes a mirror image of the left-hand side.

The central feature is a rectangular lawn around a small circular pool and fountain. Opening on to the lawn from the house is a stone terrace, which is flanked on each side by small, square borders. The terrace extends on either side into straight paths running down each side of the lawn but separated from it by a low flowering hedge. Beyond the lawn, the two paths converge into a single one, which leads beneath a tunnel of arches covered in wisteria to a small statue placed in an alcove carved out of the yew hedge forming the end boundary of the garden.

On either side of the arches are rose beds surrounded by gravel, which complement and

balance the borders at the other end of the garden by the terrace but are circular rather than square, to reflect the shape of the pool.

The narrow side borders between the paths and the boundary walls are planted up with climbers trained up and across the walls to soften them without encroaching into the limited space of the garden. To give height to the design, two fastigiate trees are planted in the far corners, just behind the rose beds, and two standard roses in containers provide lower vertical relief on the corners of the terrace.

The planting

The planting design for this garden is a compromise between relying solely on the shape and form of foliage plants and the need to provide a degree of flowering interest, bearing in mind that this is a garden to live in.

At the far end, a closely trimmed hedge of yew (*Taxus baccata*) is the backdrop for two golden fastigiate beech (*Fagus sylvatica* 'Dawyck Gold'), which are ideal in their shape and habit for a small, formal garden such as this.

The two circular rose beds are both mass-planted with the floribunda *Rosa* 'Iceberg', which makes a dramatic splash against the dark green background of the yew. This white theme is echoed, although earlier in the year, by planting the tunnel arches with *Wisteria floribunda* 'Alba', underplanted with lady's mantle (*Alchemilla mollis*) to soften the hard paving edge with its beautiful, rounded foliage.

The sharp green line of the yew hedge is repeated in the much lower hedge of dwarf box (*Buxus sempervirens* 'Suffruticosa'), which separates the circular rose beds from the path at the end of the

PLANTING PLAN

DETAIL OF WISTERIA TUNNEL

GARDEN 8 x 13m (26 x 43ft)

PLANT LIST

1 *Fagus sylvatica* 'Dawyck Gold'
2 *Taxus baccata*
3 *Alchemilla mollis*
4 *Rosa* 'Iceberg'
5 *Buxus sempervirens* 'Suffruticosa'
6 *Lavandula angustifolia* 'Hidcote'
7 *Rosa* 'The Fairy'
8 *Rosa* 'Allgold'
9 *Pelargonium* (scarlet)
10 *Rosa* 'Zéphirine Drouhin'
11 *Clematis* 'Mrs Cholmondeley'
12 *Rosa* 'Pink Perpétué'
13 *Clematis* 'Jackmanii'
14 *Rosa* 'Iceberg'
15 *Hedera helix* 'Sagittifolia'
16 *Wisteria floribunda* 'Alba'

lawn. This low hedge theme is continued around the lawn itself – leaving small gaps for access – but with a softer flowering effect created by using the dwarf lavender (*Lavandula angustifolia* 'Hidcote').

Roses and clematis, including *Rosa* 'Zéphirine Drouhin' and *Clematis* 'Mrs Cholmondeley', are used to clothe the side walls, with an underplanting of small-leaved ivy (*Hedera helix* 'Sagittifolia') covering the ground at their base and softening the edges of the stone paths.

Roses are also used elsewhere to provide colour and flower, with *Rosa* 'Allgold', a floribunda, planted *en masse* in the square borders on each side of the terrace which are edged in summer with red pelargoniums. Two standard roses (*Rosa* 'The Fairy') grow in planters on the corners of the terrace.

The features

The terrace in front of the french windows and the paths leading down the garden consist of random sized rectangular flags of York stone, which is a material ideally suited to a formal setting. This theme is continued by edging the small, circular, pre-formed fibreglass pool with dressed York stone. Within the pool a tiny fountain, powered by a submersible pump, provides movement and light in the centre of the lawn.

At the far end of the garden's long central axis, the wisteria tunnel is made up of a series of Gothic-style arches in slender, black-painted wrought iron, which show off perfectly the long, pendant flowering trusses in spring. At the very end of the tunnel, framed in an alcove created by cutting into the yew hedge, a stone statue forms a final focal point.

A warm, old red brick is used to build the boundary walls because its colour and texture are ideal for complementing both the York stone paving and the plants in the garden. Climbers on the wall are trained to grow on horizontal wires, which are set about every three or four brick courses, rather than on trellis panels, which would be too intrusive and less in keeping with the style of the garden.

VARIATIONS

▶ **Triangular variation**

The columnar trees are moved into the two narrow corners and are linked by the extended wisteria tunnel, which provides a paved route along the long boundary.

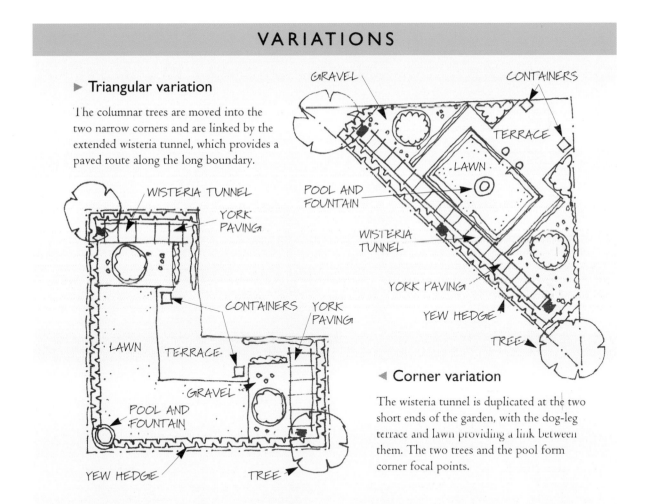

◀ **Corner variation**

The wisteria tunnel is duplicated at the two short ends of the garden, with the dog-leg terrace and lawn providing a link between them. The two trees and the pool form corner focal points.

Natural Garden

The design

Although the concept of a natural garden in the middle of a town or city may at first seem rather incongruous, in reality there is no conflict if you are able to create a garden that makes you completely unaware of what lies outside it. In a small garden it is unlikely that you will have the room to re-create to the last detail a beech woodland or damp meadow. However, it is quite possible to use one or more of these naturally occurring habitats as inspiration for you to try to create your own interpretation of them in a small area, rather than produce an exact copy.

The principal feature of this garden is its informality, with the only visible straight lines being the house walls. In such a small space, some provision must necessarily be made for the practicalities of day-to-day use and so there is an old brick patio for sitting out on, a narrow, bark-covered path, which gives access up the garden to the compost heap at the far end, and a small area of traditional mown lawn, which provides a satisfying contrast to the less-manicured parts of the garden and an alternative sitting area to the patio.

Apart from these features, the garden is broadly divided into four zones of interest: a 'woodland' area

in the far corner, consisting of a few native trees, shrubs and underplanting, which also serves to hide the compost heap; a 'meadow' of grasses and native flora, which is allowed to grow and flower before being cut, in much the same way as an old-fashioned hay meadow; a stream, flowing across the garden into a pool, which is natural in appearance, though not in construction; and finally, a generous perimeter border containing not only native plants but also varieties of a more ornamental nature in keeping with the broad concept of the design, to act as focal points and to give hot-spots of interest at different times of the year.

Apart from its visual qualities and its attraction for smaller wildlife such as insects and birds, the planting is used to hide the straight boundary fences completely and thereby create an illusion of more space. This effect is helped by the meandering path disappearing into the trees – and who knows where beyond them?

To add a touch of human scale to the scene, a tiny, rustic gazebo is tucked into the planting behind the pool, looking out over the meadow, across the stream separating it from the lawn and onto a small timber bridge where the path crosses over the stream, near its source.

The planting

The 'woodland' trees – silver birch (*Betula pendula*), mountain ash (*Sorbus aucuparia*) and bird cherry (*Prunus padus*) – are relatively modest natives that do not create excessive shade and are therefore quite suitable for most small gardens. Planted beneath these is an underlayer that closely resembles a natural woodland floor, including hazel (*Corylus avellana*), holly (*Ilex aquifolium* – one each of male and female in order to produce berries) and foxgloves (*Digitalis purpurea* Excelsior Group).

Planting in the perimeter border consists of a mixture of native shrubs more suited to open hedgerow situations, such as guelder rose (*Viburnum opulus*) and dog rose (*Rosa canina*). There are also one or two slightly more ornamental varieties to provide additional colour and flower, including mock orange (*Philadelphus* 'Beauclerk') and the Westonbirt dogwood (*Cornus alba* 'Sibirica').

PLANTING PLAN

GARDEN (short boundaries)
12 × 12m (39 × 39ft)

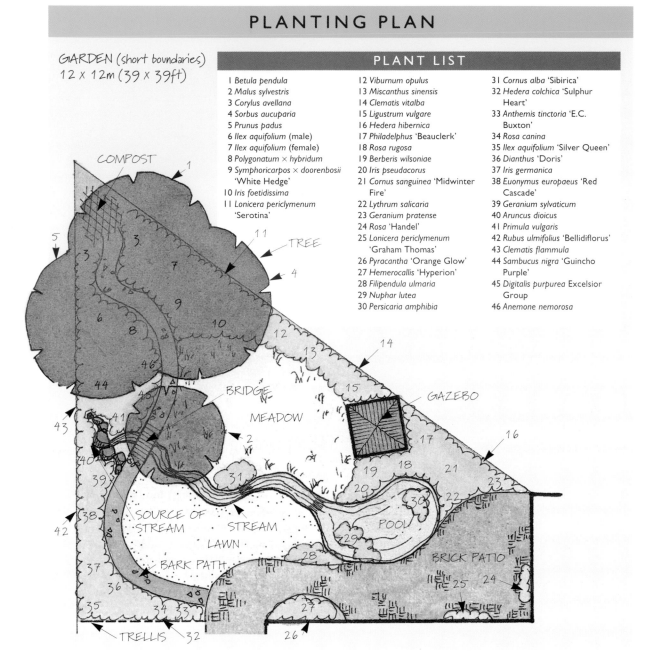

Climbers are planted along all the boundary fences to provide interest for both wildlife and humans in the form of flowers from a clematis (*Clematis flammula*), leaves from an ivy (*Hedera hibernica*, syn. *H. helix* subsp. *hibernica*) and berries and scent from honeysuckle or from woodbine (*Lonicera periclymenum* 'Serotina').

Plants commonly associated with water are planted both in and around the pool and stream – some, such as the yellow flag (*Iris pseudacorus*), are native, while others are more ornamental.

The features

The random, curved patio is made up of old bricks laid in a basketweave or herringbone pattern on a bed of sand. This gives a rather rustic feel that is somewhat reminiscent of the old paths found in traditional cottage gardens and that is, therefore, very suitable for this garden. At the far end of this brick paving, a narrow path leads to the far end of the garden and consists of chipped bark, retained along both edges by thin strips of wood, which are treated with preservative to prevent them from rotting. On soft or damp ground, the bark chips need to be laid on some form of porous membrane or even perforated black polythene to prevent them from being trodden into the soil beneath. Halfway along the path is a simple bridge crossing over the

stream, made from a couple of roughly sawn planks with a handrail of rustic larch poles on one side.

The stream and pool are constructed from overlapping sections of flexible liner. Only a slight fall is needed to create a gentle stream, although with a greater fall, more changes of level and cascades can be introduced for a more dramatic effect. A submersible pump in the pool pumps water via a buried flexible pipe to the source of the stream just beyond the bridge, where it emerges through a small pile of rocks and stones out of the ground in the manner of a spring.

The natural, rustic feel of the garden is continued in the little square gazebo with its woven hazel and willow wattle walls and thatched roof. The boundary fence, which is constructed from willow hurdles, also reflects the natural feel of the garden.

VARIATIONS

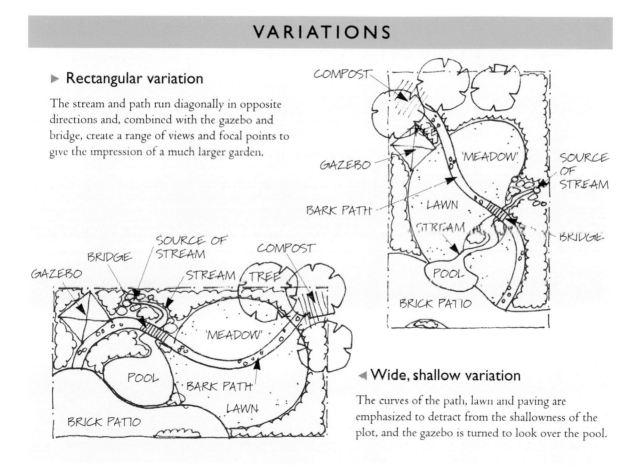

▶ **Rectangular variation**

The stream and path run diagonally in opposite directions and, combined with the gazebo and bridge, create a range of views and focal points to give the impression of a much larger garden.

◀ **Wide, shallow variation**

The curves of the path, lawn and paving are emphasized to detract from the shallowness of the plot, and the gazebo is turned to look over the pool.

Low-maintenance Garden

The design

All gardens — assuming that they are gardens in the accepted sense of the word and contain living plants — require looking after to some degree, even if it is only a matter of sweeping up dead leaves, removing faded flowers or cutting a lawn. A truly maintenance-free garden probably wouldn't be acceptable to the vast majority of the gardening population because it would, by necessity, have to be composed entirely of inanimate elements of hard landscaping and other synthetic materials. However, reducing maintenance to a minimal, and therefore an attractive, level can be achieved in any garden, from the largest plot to this pocket-handkerchief-sized example.

This garden is not only very practical and easy to look after, which means that little time need be spent on it, but it is also put together in such a way that it is attractive. In essence, the plot is divided into two.

One half focuses on a small, perfectly circular lawn, which is overlooked from an arbour in the corner, while the other half revolves around a squarish patio, leaving sufficient room in one corner for a very modest gazebo that also doubles as a garden store.

An element of privacy is given to the patio area by using wooden arches and trellis panels, which are also used to screen the bin store that is situated conveniently near the back door.

At the junction of the patio and the lawn is a small, attractive yet low-maintenance water feature, which has been carefully sited so that it becomes a focal point that can be seen from any part of the garden or indeed from the back rooms of the house.

The planting

It would be easy to fill this garden entirely with evergreen planting – shrubs, ground cover and climbers – so that not a single speck of bare soil need ever be seen again. However, this type of approach would, when compared with a more traditional type of mixed evergreen, deciduous and herbaceous planting, almost certainly limit the amount of seasonal interest available in such a small space. There are, fortunately, many deciduous varieties of plant that are quite appropriate for this style of garden because of either their dense, low-growing habit or their canopy of large, potentially weed-suppressing leaves. Cranesbill (*Geranium ibericum*), day lily (*Hemerocallis dumortieri*) and knotweed (*Persicaria amplexicaulis* 'Inverleith', syn. *Polygonum amplexicaule*) all fall into this category and have the added bonus of flowering over long periods.

Some evergreen planting is always indispensable, and this scheme includes Mexican orange blossom (*Choisya ternata*) and *Mahonia* × *media* 'Winter Sun', which contribute to the larger overall framework of the garden as well as providing attractive, scented flowers. There are also smaller examples, such as juniper (*Juniperus squamata* 'Blue Star') and *Hebe armstrongii* (syn. *H. lycopodioides* 'Aurea'), which are placed at the edges or front of the border.

With evergreens providing permanent year-round foliage, there is still room for a surprising amount of interest to be provided by deciduous shrubs, perennials and grasses throughout the year, even though space is limited. This low-maintenance style of mixed planting is made even less demanding to look after by the use of a mulch. The most effective way to use a mulch is to plant through a proprietary, rot-proof mulching fabric laid on the beds and then covered with dark bark chippings, which will not only set off the plants to perfection but will prevent any weed growth and conserve moisture.

Low-growing, leafy perennials such as *Geranium macrorrhizum*, *Lamium maculatum* 'White Nancy' and cat mint (*Nepeta* spp.) are perfect for edging low-maintenance borders.

PLANTING PLAN

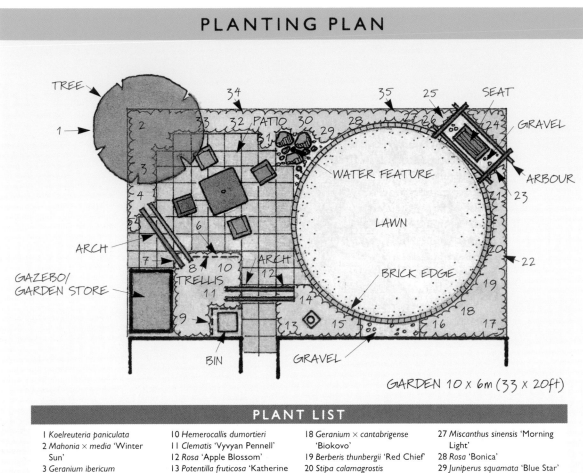

GARDEN 10 x 6m (33 x 20ft)

PLANT LIST

1 *Koelreuteria paniculata*
2 *Mahonia* × *media* 'Winter Sun'
3 *Geranium ibericum*
4 *Skimmia japonica* 'Rubella'
5 *Rosa* 'Maigold'
6 *Trachelospermum jasminoides*
7 *Clematis alpina*
8 *Berberis* × *ottawensis* 'Superba'
9 *Fargesia murieliae*

10 *Hemerocallis dumortieri*
11 *Clematis* 'Vyvyan Pennell'
12 *Rosa* 'Apple Blossom'
13 *Potentilla fruticosa* 'Katherine Dykes'
14 *Hebe pinguifolia* 'Pagei'
15 *Hosta fortunei* var. *aureomarginata*
16 *Cotoneaster microphyllus*
17 *Choisya* 'Aztec Pearl'

18 *Geranium* × *cantabrigense* 'Biokovo'
19 *Berberis thunbergii* 'Red Chief'
20 *Stipa calamagrostis*
21 *Iris sibirica* 'White Swirl'
22 *Hedera helix* 'Tricolor'
23 *Eccremocarpus scaber*
24 *Choisya ternata*
25 *Rosa* 'May Queen'
26 *Persicaria amplexicaulis* 'Inverleith'

27 *Miscanthus sinensis* 'Morning Light'
28 *Rosa* 'Bonica'
29 *Juniperus squamata* 'Blue Star'
30 *Hydrangea serrata* 'Diadem'
31 *Hebe armstrongii*
32 *Ceanothus* 'Blue Mound'
33 *Euphorbia amygdaloides* var. *robbiae*
34 *Vitis vinifera* 'Purpurea'
35 *Hedera helix* 'Chicago'

The features

The circular lawn is edged with red brick set in mortar and laid on a narrow concrete foundation to form a mowing strip that will make grass cutting much easier. The seed mix used for this lawn does not contain traditional perennial rye grass, which is much coarser and more vigorous than other varieties of lawn grass seed and would require more frequent cutting. The same red brick is also used to define the sitting area immediately beneath the arbour and the little access strip which is outside the patio doors of the house. Both of these areas are dressed in blue-grey stone chippings laid on top of the same mulching fabric that is used in the beds to prevent weed growth. Here, the mulching fabric will also help to prevent the chippings from mixing with the soil beneath.

The patio consists of square, cream-coloured imitation stone flags, which are laid on a hardcore and concrete base and then pointed with a sand–cement mortar for maximum durability and strength and to make sure there are no small cracks or gaps in which weed seeds could settle and germinate.

The arbour, arches and trellis panels are all made of sawn softwood, pressure-treated in advance with preservative to prevent rot and decay and then painted with a blue-grey stain to match the colour of the stone chippings. A similar treatment is applied to the walls of the gazebo, but a darker tone of grey is used for the roof to reduce its visual impact.

Around the garden, a hit-and-miss fence provides the boundary. It consists of horizontal boards that are nailed on to alternate sides of wooden fence posts. This is also pressure-treated before assembly and stained dark grey like the gazebo roof to act as a foil to the planting in front of it.

The water feature at the corner of the patio consists of a geyser or bubble fountain, which emerges from a sump or tank set into the ground. Rocks, boulders and pebbles are laid on top of steel reinforcing mesh, which is placed over the tank and supported by the ground around it. This type of fountain is not only attractive and safe for small children but virtually maintenance free.

As a final move towards reducing maintenance, the planting around the garden is watered by a simple irrigation system of porous pipe laid among the plants and covered by the bark mulch. The system is connected to an outside tap and can be turned on as required. Even better would be to fit a time switch to turn the system on and off for you automatically.

VARIATIONS

▶ **Rectangular variation**

The patio and arbour now lie on a diagonal axis facing across the lawn and creating a longer view, balanced by moving the tree into the other far corner.

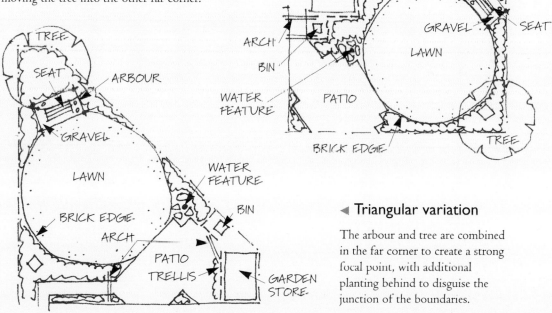

◀ **Triangular variation**

The arbour and tree are combined in the far corner to create a strong focal point, with additional planting behind to disguise the junction of the boundaries.

Beginner's Garden

The design

If you are a newcomer to gardening you will probably have two main priorities in mind for a new garden. First, you will want to have a design that not only makes the garden pleasing to look at but that will also be relatively simple to build and look after subsequently. Your second priority will probably be to keep costs down, because it is likely that the garden will have to be built to a budget.

In this example, a simple, rectangular lawn forms the hub of the design. By positioning the lawn at an angle so that it runs diagonally rather than straight up and down the plot, the whole perspective of the garden is changed for the better and a series of triangular spaces is created to accommodate other features and planting.

A patio provides a link between the house and the rest of the garden and looks out over the lawn to a small summerhouse in the opposite corner. From the patio, a narrow path runs up the left-hand side of

the lawn and around to the summerhouse. There is a wrought-iron arch at the far end of this path near the corner of the lawn, marking the entrance to a small vegetable garden and an area for storage immediately behind the summerhouse.

The vegetable garden is screened from view by an informal hedge of deciduous and evergreen shrubs running along the back edge of the path. On the opposite side of the garden to this, the triangular space created between the lawn and the boundary fence is large enough for a rotary clothes drier and a small border of planting against the fence.

The right-hand end of the patio is extended to form a staggered path that provides access to the clothes drier and around the corner of the house to the back door and beyond. This path also encloses a small space at the edge of the patio where a water feature makes an attractive focal point in the immediate foreground.

The planting

The main aim of the planting is to provide as much interest as possible throughout the year, using varieties of plant that are tolerant of a range of soil and climatic conditions, that are fairly durable and reliable and that are, of course, not too expensive to buy. Trees are essential to add height to any garden, and here a whitebeam (*Sorbus aria* 'Lutescens') and winter-flowering cherry (*Prunus* × *subhirtella* 'Autumnalis') are ideal for the purpose and will not outgrow their space and become an embarrassment. Even the smallest garden needs a planting framework, and it is provided here not only by the two trees but also by large shrubs in the perimeter border, particularly evergreens such as firethorn

A simple layout of lawn and paving combined with reliable, durable plants is the best way for beginners to get their first taste of gardening.

(*Pyracantha* 'Watereri') and barberry (*Berberis darwinii*). Other shrubs, such as variegated dogwood (*Cornus alba* 'Elegantissima') and *Escallonia* 'Apple Blossom', are included not only as framework plants but also to provide a screen to the vegetable garden.

All the plants in the garden have been selected for their relatively easy-going nature and reliability, and even over zealous or badly timed pruning – of which we are all guilty at some time in our gardening lives – is unlikely to result in anything more serious than the loss of the current year's flowers or a temporary loss of shape.

The features

All the paving in the garden, including the patio, consists of 45cm (18in) square concrete flagstones, which are buff in colour and are also slightly textured to give a non-slip finish when they are wet. The entire paving layout has been carefully worked out using whole numbers of flagstones so that no

PLANTING PLAN

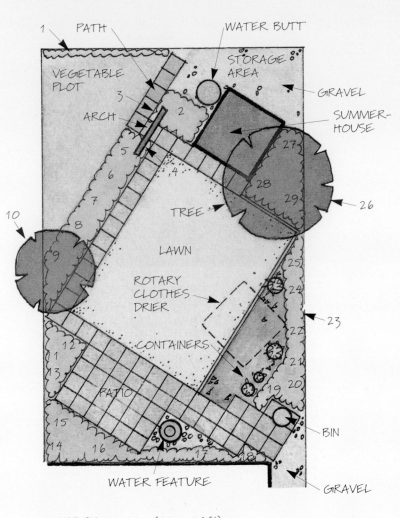

1 PATH
WATER BUTT
VEGETABLE PLOT
STORAGE AREA
GRAVEL
3
ARCH
2
SUMMER-HOUSE
5
27
6
4
28
7
29
26
8
TREE
10
9
LAWN
ROTARY CLOTHES DRIER
25
24
23
22
12
CONTAINERS
21
11
13
19 20
PATIO
15
BIN
14
16
17
18
WATER FEATURE
GRAVEL

GARDEN 7 x 11m (23 x 36ft)

PLANT LIST

1 *Clematis montana* var. *rubens*
2 *Elaeagnus* × *ebbingei* 'Limelight'
3 *Rosa* 'Paul's Scarlet Climber'
4 *Jasminum officinale*
5 *Cornus alba* 'Elegantissima'
6 *Viburnum tinus*
7 *Hydrangea macrophylla* 'Forever Pink'
8 *Escallonia* 'Apple Blossom'
9 *Lonicera nitida* 'Baggesen's Gold'
10 *Prunus* × *subhirtella* 'Autumnalis Rosea'
11 *Miscanthus sacchariflorus*
12 *Geranium* × *oxonianum* 'Wargrave Pink'
13 *Vinca minor* 'Argenteovariegata'
14 *Berberis darwinii*
15 *Ceratostigma willmottianum*
16 *Spiraea japonica* 'Gold Mound'
17 *Euonymus fortunei* 'Silver Queen'
18 *Hemerocallis* 'Stafford'
19 *Lavandula angustifolia* 'Munstead'
20 *Calamagrostis acutiflora* 'Overdam'
21 *Phygelius* × *rectus* 'African Queen'
22 *Iris* 'Frost and Flame'
23 *Hedera colchica* 'Sulphur Heart'
24 *Fuchsia magellanica* var. *gracilis* 'Aurea'
25 *Berberis thunbergii* 'Helmond Pillar'
26 *Sorbus aria* 'Lutescens'
27 *Pyracantha* 'Watereri'
28 *Hebe* 'Red Edge'
29 *Prunus laurocerasus* 'Otto Luyken'

cutting is required, which makes the laying process that much easier.

The arch at the entrance to the vegetable garden and storage area is a light, wrought-iron construction, bought ready made and painted black – some styles of arch can be acquired in one piece, while others may come in kit form in two or more sections that merely need bolting together. This particular model also has long spikes at the base so that all that is required is to push it into the firm soil on either side of the path, doing away with the need for concreting.

Where the lawn is not retained by the paving flags, an edging strip is used to prevent the grass edge from crumbling and to make mowing easier. This can be a proprietary type made from plastic or metal, or you can make your own from thin strips of wood treated with preservative and nailed or screwed to stakes, which are driven into the ground every metre or so to hold the strips firmly in place.

Both the storage area behind the summerhouse and the space around the rotary drier are mulched with gravel laid on a proprietary porous geotextile to provide an economical and durable ground cover.

The small but elegant teak-coloured summerhouse, with its hipped, shingle roof, makes a striking feature at the far end of the lawn and

doubles up in winter as a garden store for patio furniture and the barbecue. However, if the budget does not initially run to this, an alternative feature could be a small wooden arbour with a bench seat.

At the side of the patio is a self-contained water feature, which consists of nothing more than a plastic or fibreglass mould with a built-in submersible pump and a fountain head. Such features can be bought as kits, and all that is required is to sink it into the ground, making sure it is level, fill it with water – with the option of adding one or two aquatic plants and some ornamental stones – and then connect it to an external electrical supply.

VARIATIONS

▶ Long, narrow variation

The angular theme is continued, but the lawn is dog-legged to introduce more changes of direction and more viewpoints. Bringing the summerhouse forwards slightly creates a more usable storage space behind.

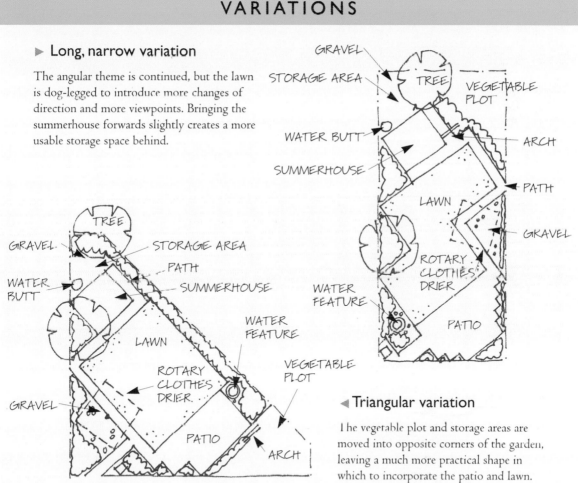

◀ Triangular variation

The vegetable plot and storage areas are moved into opposite corners of the garden, leaving a much more practical shape in which to incorporate the patio and lawn.

Sloping Garden

The design

A gently sloping garden is normally not likely to cause any great problems, and usually the most you might have to do is a small amount of regrading where a piece of level ground is needed, perhaps for a patio or around the edge of a pool.

Severe slopes, however, will call for a rather more radical solution, which normally involves terracing the garden by the creation of a series of usable level areas separated by retaining walls and linked together with steps or ramps.

What at first may appear to be an added complication in this particular example of a sloping garden is its long, narrow shape. One of the best ways of dealing with this is to divide the garden into three almost separate and roughly equal areas – a patio and deck area by the house; a circular lawn with surrounding border in the centre of the garden; and a plot for salad vegetables and soft fruit at the far, bottom end. The junctions between these three zones are appropriate places to introduce the necessary changes in level so that each part of the garden remains level. The patio and lawn are separated from each other by a brick retaining wall, which is raised above the level of the patio by 45–60cm (18–24in), creating a low safety barrier. On the far side of the lawn, the drop in level down to the salad garden is provided by a retaining edge made of logs set on end in the ground in palisade fashion.

The upper level nearest the house, the main sitting area, offers the choice of being in the sun on the patio or in dappled shade on the deck beneath a climber-covered pergola. Steps down from the patio join a stepping stone path, which runs diagonally across the lawn to another set of steps leading to the salad garden. As well as growing space, there is also room here for a small shed and a hardstanding for outside storage of a wheelbarrow and other gardening equipment.

The planting

Around the patio and deck, space for planting is confined to narrow borders in order to maximize the sitting area. Consequently, planting is limited to the use of climbers, such as passion flower (*Passiflora caerulea*) and *Clematis* 'Madame Julia Correvon', growing up and over the pergola, and wall shrubs, such as *Ceanothus impressus*, which can be kept trimmed to whatever size is required.

On the middle terrace, around the circular lawn, planting consists of a framework of taller shrubs and trees, with smaller shrubs and perennials used as infill and edging. In small, narrow gardens such as this, the selection of trees suitable for the situation is most important, and a fastigiate crab apple (*Malus tschonoskii*) and red hawthorn (*Crataegus laevigata* 'Paul's Scarlet', syn. *C. laevigata* 'Coccinea Plena') are good choices here because although they will not outgrow their allotted space they nevertheless provide valuable height. Flowering interest in this part of the garden peaks in summer, and montbretia (*Crocosmia × crocosmiiflora*), scabious (*Scabiosa caucasica* 'Clive Greaves') and *Potentilla fruticosa* 'Abbotswood' have been selected for their long flowering periods. Climbers are used to soften the boundary fences, including potato vine (*Solanum jasminoides* 'Album'), chosen for its masses of small white flowers, and *Actinidia kolomikta*, chosen for its striking pink, cream and green foliage.

Steps and retaining walls can be used to create level areas for planting and other purposes in a sloping garden.

The features

The patio consists of square, pre-cast concrete flagstones with a textured finish of exposed aggregate. For a warmer effect the colour of the aggregate should be a mixture of buff, pale brown and cream, for example, rather than colder blues and greys.

Adjoining this patio is the deck, which is constructed from narrow lengths – approximately 7.5cm (3in) wide – of sawn, pressure-treated softwood nailed to joists in the manner of a wooden

PLANTING PLAN

GARDEN 6.5 × 15m (21 × 49ft)

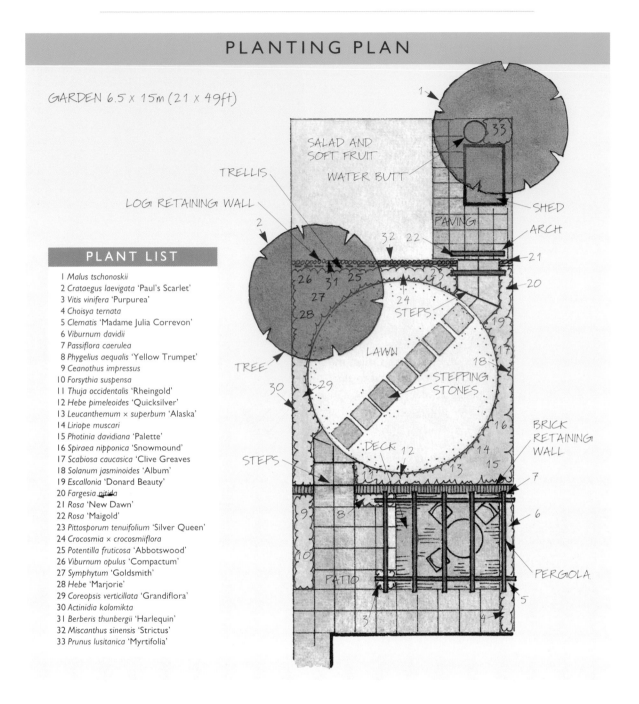

SALAD AND
SOFT FRUIT

WATER BUTT

TRELLIS

LOG RETAINING WALL

PAVING

SHED

ARCH

33

21

20

32 22

19

17

18

24
STEPS

STEPPING
STONES

LAWN

16

TREE

BRICK
RETAINING
WALL

30

29

7

STEPS

DECK 12

14

15

13

6

9

8

5

10

PERGOLA

PATIO

3

4

PLANT LIST

1 *Malus tschonoskii*
2 *Crataegus laevigata* 'Paul's Scarlet'
3 *Vitis vinifera* 'Purpurea'
4 *Choisya ternata*
5 *Clematis* 'Madame Julia Correvon'
6 *Viburnum davidii*
7 *Passiflora caerulea*
8 *Phygelius aequalis* 'Yellow Trumpet'
9 *Ceanothus impressus*
10 *Forsythia suspensa*
11 *Thuja occidentalis* 'Rheingold'
12 *Hebe pimeleoides* 'Quicksilver'
13 *Leucanthemum × superbum* 'Alaska'
14 *Liriope muscari*
15 *Photinia davidiana* 'Palette'
16 *Spiraea nipponica* 'Snowmound'
17 *Scabiosa caucasica* 'Clive Greaves'
18 *Solanum jasminoides* 'Album'
19 *Escallonia* 'Donard Beauty'
20 *Fargesia nitida*
21 *Rosa* 'New Dawn'
22 *Rosa* 'Maigold'
23 *Pittosporum tenuifolium* 'Silver Queen'
24 *Crocosmia × crocosmiiflora*
25 *Potentilla fruticosa* 'Abbotswood'
26 *Viburnum opulus* 'Compactum'
27 *Symphytum* 'Goldsmith'
28 *Hebe* 'Marjorie'
29 *Coreopsis verticillata* 'Grandiflora'
30 *Actinidia kolomikta*
31 *Berberis thunbergii* 'Harlequin'
32 *Miscanthus sinensis* 'Strictus'
33 *Prunus lusitanica* 'Myrtifolia'

floor, leaving a slight gap between each piece, which will allow rainwater to drain through. The deck is unstained and is left to weather down to a natural silver-grey finish. In contrast, the wooden pergola, which is also made from treated softwood, is stained

a dark oak or similar colour in order to set off the flowers and foliage of the climbers that are growing up and over it.

The retaining wall between the patio and lawn is built from a red walling brick, and the same type of brick is also used for the step risers throughout the garden. The step treads and the stepping stone path are made from flagstones similar to those used in the patio.

To provide a degree of separation between the ornamental lawn and the more functional garden for salad vegetables and soft fruit beyond there is a narrow arch spanning the steps, and this is made from timber to match both the style and the colour of the pergola.

The change in ground level at this point is achieved by means of a log retaining wall, which consists of peeled and pressure-treated softwood logs set on end, side by side, in a narrow bed of concrete. The concrete is allowed to strengthen before the soil behind the logs is replaced, and a sheet of heavy-duty black polythene is fixed to the back face of the wall at the same time so that fine soil is not washed through any gaps.

As well as space set aside for growing crops in the salad and soft fruit garden, there is an area of hardstanding consisting of plain, concrete flagstones, which provide not only a level base for a small garden shed but also a clean, firm area for a water butt and other ancillary garden items that can be stored in the open.

VARIATIONS

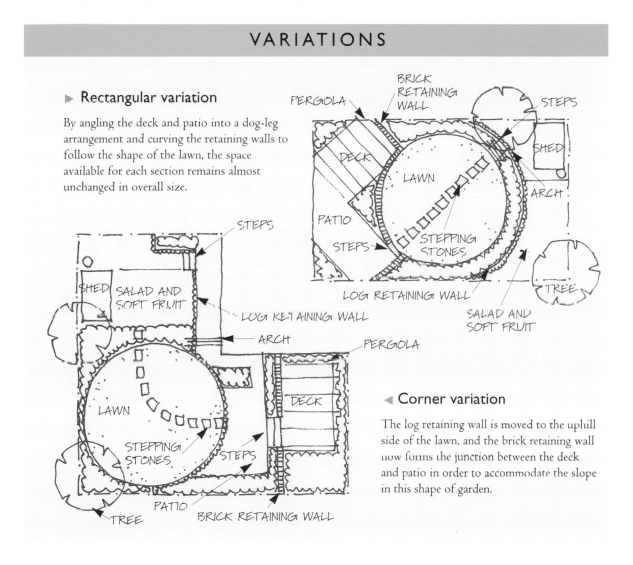

▶ Rectangular variation

By angling the deck and patio into a dog-leg arrangement and curving the retaining walls to follow the shape of the lawn, the space available for each section remains almost unchanged in overall size.

◀ Corner variation

The log retaining wall is moved to the uphill side of the lawn, and the brick retaining wall now forms the junction between the deck and patio in order to accommodate the slope in this shape of garden.

Cottage Garden

The design

Traditional cottage gardens arose originally out of the need to produce fruit, vegetables, herbs and flowers primarily for eating and medicinal purposes. You could say, therefore, that they were more a product of evolution than of design.

Present-day pressures and needs are, however, somewhat different, and while the visual attractions of a cottage garden are no less, achieving the same effect requires a rather more organized approach by way of a plan, and this is especially important where garden space is limited.

By their nature, cottage gardens are informal and the design therefore sets out to emulate this characteristic with a curving, almost circular patio leading to a narrow path that meanders across and up the garden, eventually leading to a small potting shed next to which, and screened from the rest of the garden by rustic trellis, is a kitchen garden.

The patio opens out onto a central lawn on which sits a birdbath – although a statue or sundial would be equally appropriate – and continuing the rustic theme is a small gazebo, which is tucked away under a tree to the side of the path and looks back over the lawn. Just to the left-hand side of the patio is a small, natural-looking pool, around the back of which the path wanders, passing as it does so beneath three rustic arches built in the same style as the trellis screen.

The planting

The informal design of this garden, with its sweeping curves and soft edges, largely disguises the fact that it is a small and rectangular plot, and covering the boundaries with soft planting also helps. A selection of climbers, ranging from perfoliate honeysuckle (*Lonicera caprifolium*) to *Clematis montana* 'Elizabeth', is used here, and the rustic screens are treated similarly, with climbers such as *Rosa* 'Mermaid' and golden hop (*Humulus lupulus* 'Aureus') providing a backdrop and separating the ornamental part of the garden in front from the more functional one behind.

Scent is traditionally a feature of cottage gardens, and in this scheme it is to be found both in climbers on the arches — woodbine (*Lonicera periclymenum* 'Belgica'), for example — and also throughout the borders in both shrubs — such as *Viburnum* × *burkwoodii* — and perennials — such as pinks (*Dianthus* 'Doris').

Even in a small garden, trees are valuable for their height and scale. This is provided by a winter-flowering cherry (*Prunus* × *subhirtella* 'Autumnalis'), a mountain ash (*Sorbus aucuparia*) and an elegant form of birch (*Betula pendula* 'Tristis'), all of which have light, delicate foliage and will not, therefore, create heavy pockets of shade.

The perimeter border contains a mixture of shrubs, perennials and grasses, which blend together and create a familiar cottage garden feel. Old favourites, such as the tall bearded iris (*Iris* 'Jane Phillips') and *Delphinium* Black Knight Group, are planted alongside less obvious but equally effective varieties such as golden oat grass (*Stipa gigantea*) and knotweed (*Persicaria bistorta* 'Superba').

The bed around the pool includes plants that are often associated with damp or wet areas, such as *Hosta* 'Big Daddy', meadowsweet (*Filipendula ulmaria*) and *Astilbe* × *arendsii* 'Snowdrift', and that also fit into the overall planting theme.

Annuals are, of course, as much a part of cottage gardens as herbaceous perennials and climbing roses, and while some are planted in a variety of containers sitting on the patio, others are allowed to self-seed in the beds and borders where they can be thinned to leave as many as are required.

Even in a small space, the essence of a cottage garden can be captured with plants such as foxgloves (*Digitalis*), lupins (*Lupinus*), mock orange (*Philadelphus coronarius*) and climbing roses.

The features

The crazy-paved patio is made from randomly shaped pieces of York stone, and because it will be well used, the joints between the pieces are filled and pointed with a sand–cement mortar for strength and to maintain a level, even surface. Near the edge, however, one or two joints can be left unpointed and filled instead with fine soil to allow a few small, self-seeded annuals, such as alyssum, to grow each year.

The path is made from reclaimed red bricks, which are laid in a herringbone pattern that is reminiscent of an old garden. These bricks are pushed tight up against each other and fine, dry sand is then brushed over them to fill any tiny cracks that may be left. Although you are bound to get one or two weeds germinating in these sand-filled gaps, by sprinkling a few mixed annual seeds along the edges of the path you can also encourage more desirable flowering plants to grow there if you wish.

Round, peeled larch poles are used to make both the simple arches over the path near the pool and the

PLANTING PLAN

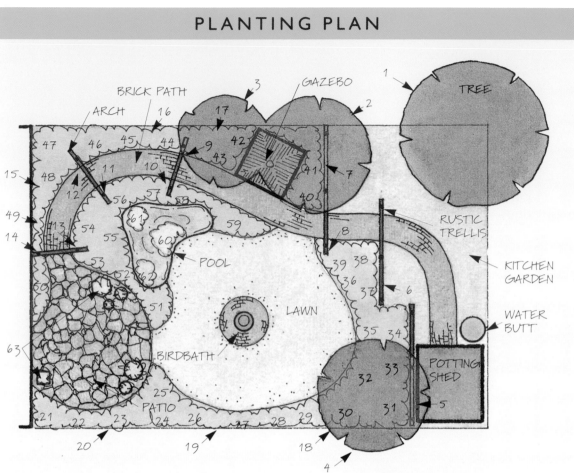

GARDEN 8 x 12m (26 x 39ft)

PLANT LIST

1 *Malus* 'Bramley's Seedling'
2 *Prunus* × *subhirtella* 'Autumnalis'
3 *Sorbus aucuparia*
4 *Betula pendula* 'Tristis'
5 *Clematis flammula*
6 *Rosa* 'Mermaid'
7 *Humulus lupulus* 'Aureus'
8 *Rosa* 'Zéphirine Drouhin'
9 *Clematis* 'Nelly Moser'
10 *Jasminum officinale*
11 *Rosa* 'Pink Perpétué'
12 *Clematis* 'Marie Boisselot'
13 *Hedera helix* 'Angularis Aurea'
14 *Lonicera periclymenum* 'Belgica'
15 *Pyracantha* 'Soleil d'Or'
16 *Vitis vinifera*
17 *Lonicera caprifolium*

18 *Lonicera japonica* 'Aureoreticulata'
19 *Clematis montana* 'Elizabeth'
20 *Rosa* 'Meg'
21 *Berberis thunbergii* f. *atropurpurea*
22 *Helleborus argutifolius*
23 *Hemerocallis* 'Bonanza'
24 *Philadelphus coronarius* 'Aureus'
25 *Geranium* 'Johnson's Blue'
26 *Lupinus* 'Noble Maiden'
27 *Stipa gigantea*
28 *Aster amellus* 'King George'
29 *Skimmia japonica* 'Veitchii'
30 *Hydrangea* 'Preziosa'
31 *Ilex aquifolium* 'Pyramidalis'
32 *Dicentra eximia*

33 *Digitalis purpurea* Excelsior Group
34 *Deutzia* × *hybrida* 'Mont Rose'
35 *Iris* 'Jane Phillips'
36 *Dianthus* 'Doris'
37 *Delphinium* Black Knight Group
38 *Cotinus* 'Grace'
39 *Solidago* 'Queenie'
40 *Campanula persicifolia* var. *alba*
41 *Aucuba japonica* 'Variegata'
42 *Viburnum* × *burkwoodii*
43 *Geranium renardii*
44 *Sidalcea* 'Rose Queen'
45 *Fuchsia magellanica*
46 *Rosa glauca*
47 *Fremontodendron* 'California Glory'

48 *Kniphofia* 'Percy's Pride'
49 *Lavandula angustifolia*
50 *Agapanthus campanulatus* var. *albidus*
51 *Iris sibirica* 'Tropic Night'
52 *Hosta* 'Big Daddy'
53 *Eryngium variifolium*
54 *Crocosmia* 'Lucifer'
55 *Iris pseudacorus* 'Variegata'
56 *Filipendula ulmaria*
57 *Monarda* 'Cambridge Scarlet'
58 *Astilbe* × *arendsii* 'Snowdrift'
59 *Persicaria bistorta* 'Superba'
60 *Iris laevigata* 'Variegata'
61 *Caltha palustris* var. *alba*
62 *Lobelia cardinalis*
63 Herbs in containers

rustic trellis towards the back of the garden. The poles can be simply nailed together, and any joints need be only roughly sawn to fit as this will add to the overall rustic effect. Remember, however, that the lower ends of the posts for the arches and trellis must be treated with preservative to prevent them from rotting when they are secured in the ground. The framework of the small, square gazebo is assembled from the same type of pole and is finished off with a thatched roof of straw or reed to complete the effect.

Rather than placing the birdbath or other feature directly onto the lawn, it is put on a small circle of

crazy York stone paving, which acts as a mowing strip for easy grass cutting, provided that the level of this paving is set 10–15mm (about $\frac{1}{2}$in) below the level of the turf to avoid damaging the mower blades.

The pool is a pre-formed fibreglass or plastic moulding, which is simple to install by digging a hole to a suitable depth and placing it in the hole on a bed of soft sand. Make sure it is absolutely level before backfilling around with fine soil. The thin, rigid edges of such pre-formed pools are ideal for allowing grass and plants to grow right up to the water's edge for a natural appearance.

VARIATIONS

▶ Square variation

The lawn is made a more circular shape with the intention of masking the formal lines of the plot. The gazebo forms a strong focal point diagonally opposite the patio to emphasize this effect.

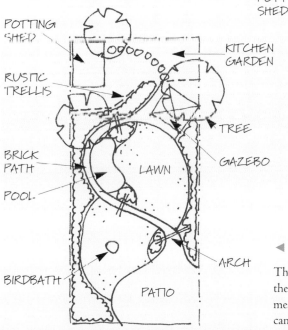

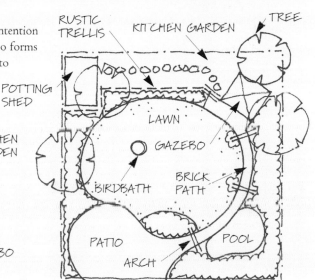

◀ Long, narrow variation

The gazebo is brought forward to make space behind for the kitchen garden. The garden is divided into two by the meandering path and arches, masking the tunnel effect that can characterize narrow plots like this.

Roof Garden

The design

With land at a premium in many towns and cities, the use of flat roof spaces to create gardens in the sky is becoming more and more attractive. There are three principal factors that need to be considered before building a roof garden. First, you must check that the roof is strong enough for you to build a garden there in the first place; second, a suitable type and amount of growing medium – whether it's soil, peat, rockwool or other material – must be selected for the purpose; finally, the design of garden and choice of plants should take into account the greater extremes of weather often experienced at a higher level around buildings, particularly the effect of the wind.

Keeping the weight of all the materials used in creating a roof garden to an absolute minimum is a good policy to adopt, not only to ensure that you keep the overall loading to an acceptable level, but also because all these materials will have to be transported up to the roof by some means, which in many cases will be by hand.

In this example, a central area for sitting is laid out in very thin slate paving, with lightweight timber decks at each side. Above each deck is a pergola arrangement, with the outermost posts of the structure fixed directly to the load-bearing perimeter walls. Swirling winds and eddies are commonly

Positioning them around the strongest part of a roof, the edge, makes it possible to grow heavy plants like these birch trees (*Betula pendula*).

found immediately around buildings, and in order to provide shelter from these, trellis panels are fixed between the perimeter posts of both pergolas to break up the strong air flows. This arrangement will ensure that, regardless of the wind direction, there will always be at least one relatively sheltered spot somewhere in the garden, yet it still leaves uninterrupted the distant view directly from the building across the centre of the roof.

Planting is largely contained within narrow raised wooden planters and one or two individual containers located around the edge of the roof where it is strongest, with the exception of two climbers, one in the centre of each pergola.

A statue and fibreglass pool are similarly located away from the centre of the roof, which leaves a very useful uncluttered area of paving and decking to enable seats and other garden furniture to be moved into the most comfortable location according to the sun and prevailing wind at the time.

The planting

The planting has been selected to provide sufficient screening and shelter (particularly by the climbers) without becoming too dense and thereby cutting out light from the garden space and, indeed, the house. To achieve this, the climbers on the trellis panels are all deciduous so that in the generally shorter, gloomier days of winter, the maximum amount of light and low sun can penetrate through the leafless stems. Roses (*Rosa* 'Aloha' and *R.* 'Danse du Feu'), golden hop (*Humulus lupulus* 'Aureus') and honeysuckle (*Lonicera* × *heckrottii* 'Gold Flame') are all included, not only for this purpose, but also because they will tolerate the relatively exposed nature of a roof garden.

PLANTING PLAN

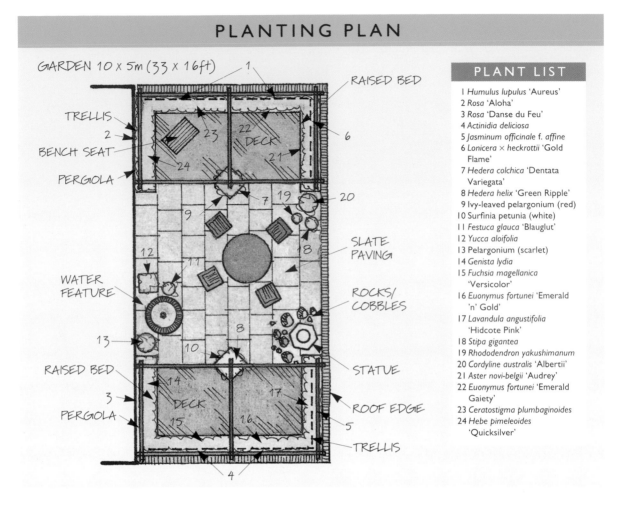

GARDEN 10 x 5m (33 x 16ft)

TRELLIS

BENCH SEAT

PERGOLA

WATER FEATURE

RAISED BED

PERGOLA

RAISED BED

DECK

SLATE PAVING

ROCKS/ COBBLES

STATUE

ROOF EDGE

TRELLIS

PLANT LIST

1 *Humulus lupulus* 'Aureus'
2 *Rosa* 'Aloha'
3 *Rosa* 'Danse du Feu'
4 *Actinidia deliciosa*
5 *Jasminum officinale* f. *affine*
6 *Lonicera × heckrottii* 'Gold Flame'
7 *Hedera colchica* 'Dentata Variegata'
8 *Hedera helix* 'Green Ripple'
9 Ivy-leaved pelargonium (red)
10 Surfinia petunia (white)
11 *Festuca glauca* 'Blauglut'
12 *Yucca aloifolia*
13 Pelargonium (scarlet)
14 *Genista lydia*
15 *Fuchsia magellanica* 'Versicolor'
16 *Euonymus fortunei* 'Emerald 'n' Gold'
17 *Lavandula angustifolia* 'Hidcote Pink'
18 *Stipa gigantea*
19 *Rhododendron yakushimanum*
20 *Cordyline australis* 'Albertii'
21 *Aster novi-belgii* 'Audrey'
22 *Euonymus fortunei* 'Emerald Gaiety'
23 *Ceratostigma plumbaginoides*
24 *Hebe pimeleoides* 'Quicksilver'

Evergreen foliage is not completely absent, though, and is provided by two ivies (*Hedera colchica* 'Dentata Variegata' and *H. helix* 'Green Ripple') growing up the inner central posts of the two pergolas. They are trimmed annually to maintain them as vertical columns of foliage and to prevent them from growing across the tops of the pergolas and casting too much heavy shade.

In the perimeter planters a selection of lower growing plants is used to provide both foliage and flower interest. All the varieties here have been chosen because of their tolerance to the extremes of microclimate often found on roofs. Some, such as blue fescue (*Festuca glauca* 'Blauglut') and *Euonymus fortunei* 'Emerald 'n' Gold', provide year-round interest with their evergreen foliage, while others,

like *Fuchsia magellanica* 'Versicolor', provide summer flowers over a long period.

Hot-spots of additional summer colour are added by planting up containers with red pelargoniums and white petunias, and these have the added benefit that they can be moved to any desired position.

The features

To save weight, the central patio is made from rectangular pieces of very thin, blue-grey, paving-quality slate. These pieces are fixed to the roof with a proprietary waterproof adhesive rather than a more traditional sand–cement mortar, which would be much heavier. To the sides of this area, the naturally weathered decking consists of very thin battens of pressure-treated softwood, laid and fixed diagonally to shallow, similarly treated wooden bearers in the manner of a duckboard. The whole deck structure is restrained and prevented from moving sideways by the raised wooden planters and the edge of the slate paving and, provided it is even, it does not, therefore, need to be fixed directly to the surface of the roof.

The perimeter planters are made out of vertical softwood boards or planks, pressure-treated like the decking, and stained blue-grey to complement the colour of the slate. Heavy duty polythene or builder's damp-proof membrane is fixed to the back of the boards to help retain moisture in the soil-less compost used for planting and also to prevent damp from staining the outer face of the wood.

Similarly treated and coloured timber is used for the pergolas and the square-patterned trellis panels. Wherever possible, the posts for these are bolted

either to the balustrade wall or the building itself to provide extra strength and rigidity and to take as much load as possible away from the centre of the roof.

Ornamentation is provided by a statue surrounded by a collection of various white rocks and stones, and a circular white fibreglass pool just in front and to the side of the patio doors. A tiny submersible pump in the pool powers a bubble or geyser fountain, which is much more appropriate than a taller jet that would be more likely to be blown around by the wind.

One final important detail is to ensure that the edge of the garden not enclosed by trellis is made safe and secure, particularly if the balustrade wall is lower than about 90cm (3ft), by installing some form of horizontal guard rail, which in this case is made from timber to match the pergola and trellis.

VARIATIONS

▶ Rectangular variation

The two pergolas and trellis are placed in diagonally opposite corners so that, regardless of wind direction, there will always be a protected sitting area.

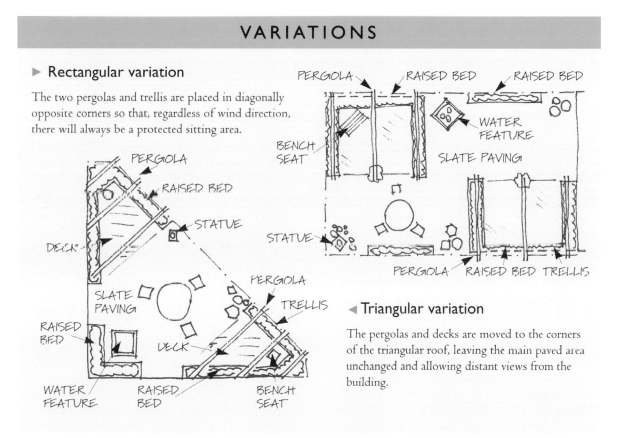

◀ Triangular variation

The pergolas and decks are moved to the corners of the triangular roof, leaving the main paved area unchanged and allowing distant views from the building.

Container Garden

The design

Growing plants in containers is an area of gardening that has now extended well beyond the traditional use of annuals such as pelargoniums and lobelia and their like, since virtually any plant – from alpines, bulbs, heathers, grasses and perennials to shrubs and even small trees – can be successfully grown this way, provided that the right cultural conditions are provided.

Container planting can really come into its own in a small garden, however, where every plant must make a contribution to the overall picture. In a limited space, having the ability quickly to change an effect – by replacing pots of annual summer bedding with plants such as skimmia and purple ornamental

cabbage for winter effect, for example – or the flexibility of being able to move plants around for practical purposes or even on a whim are valuable qualities.

There are situations where every single plant in a garden could be planted in a container, particularly in tiny spaces or where ground conditions are unsuitable for normal planting, such as on a balcony. However, this can become very time-consuming and labour intensive on anything other than a small scale, particularly where a lot of seasonal replanting is needed. The design of this small, square garden, therefore, sets out to create a framework of hard landscape features and permanent peripheral planting of trees, shrubs and climbers, which will act as a setting and backdrop for a whole range of containers and plants to put in them.

Essentially, the design revolves around a central area of gravel, which encloses a dramatic rock and water feature. Three rectangular areas of brick paving are linked together in a continuous chain by a generous path of York stone flags. The largest of these brick areas forms a patio by the house, the central one provides the base for a small arbour, and the smallest of the three is used simply as a space in which to display particular pots or ornaments according to the season or personal preference.

Two arches, one each side of the patio, create a slight sense of separation and enclosure to this area, where a solid wall or fence would be too oppressive.

Permanent planting around the garden consists primarily of shrubs and small trees planted in the far corners, together with hardy climbers, which are trained up trellis panels mounted on the boundary walls and provide a framework against which the containers can be displayed to their best effect.

The planting

As well as giving valuable height at the far end of the garden, the two trees — mountain ash (*Sorbus* 'Joseph Rock') and Himalayan birch (*Betula utilis* var. *jacquemontii*) — are attractive in their own right, with their respective features of yellow autumn berries and white bark in winter.

The perimeter shrub planting contains a generous proportion of evergreens, some of which are chosen predominantly for their habit and foliage effects, including variegated Portugal laurel (*Prunus lusitanica* 'Variegata'), and others more for their striking flowers, such as *Rhododendron* 'Cynthia'. Many of these shrubs have the potential to become relatively large specimens, which is essential if the garden is not to appear fragmented and bitty, but all are amenable to some degree of pruning so that the right balance of size and scale can be maintained throughout.

Containers can be used to grow a range of plants, not just traditional annuals. Some containers, like this half barrel, can make wonderful small water features.

The garden boundaries are softened and hidden partly by the perimeter shrubs but also by a number of climbers, which are trained onto trellis panels attached directly to the walls. These are all, in the main, strong-growing varieties, which will provide good cover in a comparatively short time — ivy (*Hedera helix* 'Buttercup'), honeysuckle (*Lonicera periclymenum* 'Graham Thomas') and jasmine (*Jasminum stephanense*), but again they will respond to quite heavy pruning where necessary to keep them in check.

Planted in various containers placed on the brick, stone and gravel areas throughout the garden is a wide range of plants, both large and small, including hardy and tender varieties. In cold climates the latter will need to be overwintered in a conservatory or other suitable protected location if they are to be retained for the following year. Some plants, such as *Hosta* 'Frances Williams' and New Zealand flax (*Phormium tenax* Purpureum Group), are chosen specifically for their dramatic foliage and form, while others, such as oleander (*Nerium oleander*) and pelargoniums, are included for their dazzling flower

PLANTING PLAN

PLANT LIST

1 *Sorbus* 'Joseph Rock'
2 *Elaeagnus × ebbingei*
3 *Prunus lusitanica* 'Variegata'
4 *Hedera helix* 'Buttercup'
5 *Betula utilis* var. *jacquemontii*
6 *Aucuba japonica* 'Crotonifolia'
7 *Osmanthus × burkwoodii*
8 *Camellia japonica* 'Adolphe Audusson'
9 *Lonicera periclymenum* 'Graham Thomas'
10 *Photinia × fraseri* 'Rubens'
11 *Pyracantha* 'Orange Glow'
12 *Euonymus japonicus* 'Ovatus Aureus'
13 *Viburnum tinus* 'Gwenllian'
14 *Pittosporum tobira*
15 *Rhododendron* 'Cynthia'
16 *Jasminum × stephanense*
17 *Berberis × stenophylla*
18 *Rosa* 'Schoolgirl'
19 *Clematis* 'Rouge Cardinal'
20 *Ampelopsis glandulosa* var. *brevipedunculata* 'Elegans'
21 *Clematis* 'Henryi'
22 *Rosa* 'Albertine'
23 *Trachelospermum jasminoides* 'Variegatum'
24 *Rosa* 'Handel'
25 *Jasminum officinale* 'Argenteovariegatum'
26 *Clematis alpina* subsp. *sibirica* 'White Moth'
27 *Hedera helix* 'Oro di Bogliasco'

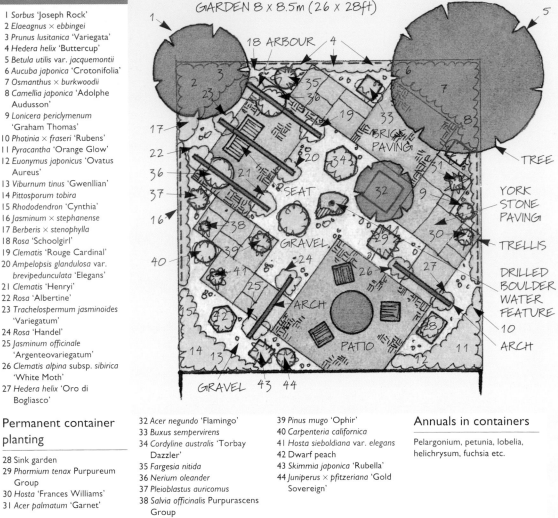

GARDEN 8 x 8.5m (26 x 28ft)

18 ARBOUR
BRICK PAVING
SEAT
GRAVEL
ARCH
PATIO
GRAVEL 43 44

TREE
YORK STONE PAVING
TRELLIS
DRILLED BOULDER WATER FEATURE
ARCH

Permanent container planting

28 Sink garden
29 *Phormium tenax* Purpureum Group
30 *Hosta* 'Frances Williams'
31 *Acer palmatum* 'Garnet'

32 *Acer negundo* 'Flamingo'
33 *Buxus sempervirens*
34 *Cordyline australis* 'Torbay Dazzler'
35 *Fargesia nitida*
36 *Nerium oleander*
37 *Pleioblastus auricomus*
38 *Salvia officinalis* Purpurascens Group

39 *Pinus mugo* 'Ophir'
40 *Carpenteria californica*
41 *Hosta sieboldiana* var. *elegans*
42 Dwarf peach
43 *Skimmia japonica* 'Rubella'
44 *Juniperus × pfitzeriana* 'Gold Sovereign'

Annuals in containers

Pelargonium, petunia, lobelia, helichrysum, fuchsia etc.

displays over long periods of time. The range in the size of both containers and plants is well illustrated by comparing the tree-sized box elder (*Acer negundo* 'Flamingo') in its large, square planter with the tiny sedums and saxifrages in their small, clay half-pans. In fact, the only real limiting factor to the size of the container is whether you will need to move it at some stage in the future.

The features

Bricks for the paving are chosen to match the colour of the boundary wall, and are laid in a basketweave style, which is well suited to square and rectangular shapes. The path linking these brick areas consists of York stone flags, with large pieces being used where possible in order to leave spaces at the corners on which to stand some of the smaller containers. Joints about 20mm (¾in) wide are left between adjacent flagstones and are filled with a fine gravel or grit.

The two arches on each side of the patio are made from heavy, square-sawn oak posts and cross-rails, left untreated and allowed to weather naturally. Oak is also used for the cross-rails of the arbour, but these are set on the top of narrow brick piers, rather than posts, which are built to match the surrounding walls. On the walls themselves, the trellis panels used are made from very simple square-sectioned wood, left unstained because they will very quickly become covered and hidden from view by the climbers they support and their appearance is not critical.

Creamy white gravel forms the ground cover over the central part of the garden and also between the

outer edge of the path and the perimeter shrub planting. It is laid on top of a proprietary membrane or geotextile, so that weeds will be prevented from growing and the gravel will not become mixed into the soil.

The focal point of this part of the garden is a large rock, selected to match the gravel, which is drilled vertically to allow water from a plastic tank underneath it to be pumped up through the central hole and over its face by means of a submersible pump. The rock is suspended on steel reinforcing bars and mesh laid across the top of the tank and supported by the surrounding ground. Finishing this off with a layer of membrane allows the gravel to be spread over it right up to the base of the rock, thereby hiding the tank and steelwork beneath.

VARIATIONS

▶ Long, narrow variation

The plot is too narrow for a 'circular' route, so the path is angled from right to left and back again, linking the patio, arbour and brick sitting area at the far end of the garden. The *Acer negundo* 'Flamingo' is kept central to retain an element of surprise behind it.

▼ Wide, shallow variation

The far corners are softened by the two trees to disguise the rectangular nature of the plot. The water feature becomes the central focal point, with the path angled to create a 'circular' route around the garden.

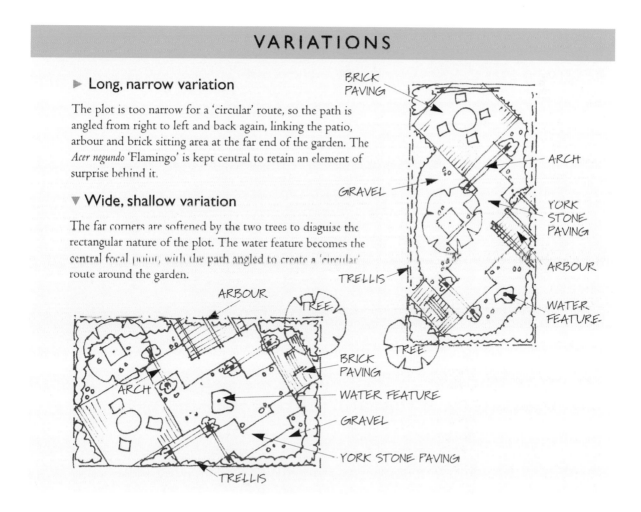

Trellis Garden

The design

In most large gardens there is generally enough room to create an effective screen of large shrubs and trees if a degree of privacy or enclosure is needed. However, the demands on space in a small garden mean that generous planting on such a scale is not always possible because of the amount of room it would take up. A simple solution to this problem is to build walls or fences on which climbers and other wall plants can be grown and trained up to suit the space available, and that will require only narrow beds or borders for planting in, leaving more area available for other features such as a lawn and patio.

In many cases this can be very effective. One drawback of walls and close-boarded or panel-type fences, though, is the fact that because they are solid, they are more likely to cut out a lot of light, particularly when they are used to enclose a small area. Using some form of perforated screen, such as trellis, overcomes this problem because it not only provides a vertical surface that is strong enough to support suitable plants, but it will still allow a certain amount of light and air through, which are appreciated by both plants and people.

This small corner garden cleverly uses trellis not only in order to save space but also as a means of dividing it into three distinct parts. There is a patio area in front of the french windows, incorporating a small barbecue and giving access down the side of the house to the front garden. On the other side of the patio, a dog-leg arrangement of trellis panels leads into a second area while still hiding it from view. This area is entirely surrounded by trellis and narrow borders, and consists of a central lawn with a small, partly octagonal summerhouse in the far corner looking out over the lawn. A stepping stone path links the patio area across the corner of this lawn to a third area, which is more utilitarian and contains a shed, a greenhouse, space for refuse bins and even a small plot for growing a few vegetables and salad crops. Trellis is also used for the boundary fence around the plot as well as for the divisions within it, ensuring that the whole garden remains as light and airy as possible.

The planting

The principal philosophy behind the planting is to use climbers on the trellis to provide height and screening, and to use lower planting of small shrubs and perennials at the base of the climbers to soften the straight edges and extend the period of interest. Climbers in this garden are predominantly deciduous so that in winter, when the sun is lower and the day length is less, as much light as possible is allowed to penetrate into the garden, but leaving enough bare stems to provide some degree of screening. Purple grape vine (*Vitis vinifera* 'Purpurea'), *Actinidia kolomikta* and *Clematis alpina* 'Frances Rivis', for example, are all suitable for this purpose. Evergreen climbers are used, however, in one or two places, such as an ivy (*Hedera canariensis* 'Gloire de Marengo') along the side boundary of the patio, and another ivy (*Hedera colchica* 'Sulphur Heart') and *Trachelospermum asiaticum* at the entrance to the utility area, where more permanent and effective screening is desirable. These can all be trimmed regularly so that they remain within bounds.

A limited number of slightly larger shrubs are used, particularly in the corners of the lawn border – *Choisya ternata* 'Sundance' and *Potentilla fruticosa* 'Abbotswood' – and the patio area – *Hypericum* 'Hidcote' – where some extra height and depth is needed to prevent the planting from looking too flat.

Trellis can be used to support wonderful climbing plants like these roses, yet only take up a small amount of valuable ground space.

PLANTING PLAN

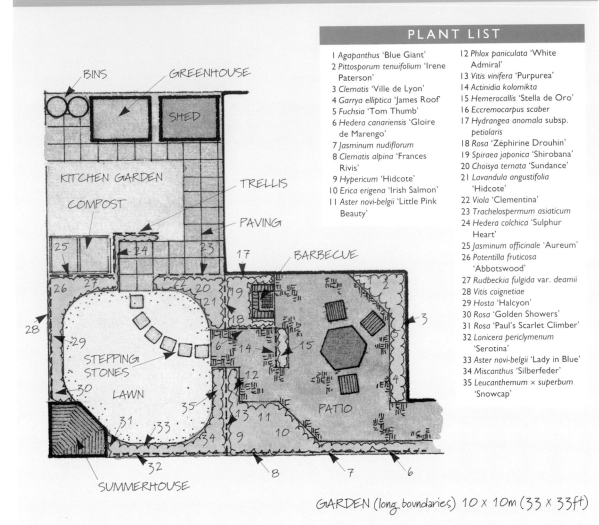

BINS GREENHOUSE

SHED

KITCHEN GARDEN

COMPOST

TRELLIS

PAVING

25 24 23 17 BARBECUE

26 27 22 20 19
28 21 18
29 6 14 15
STEPPING
STONES 12
30 LAWN 2 3
35 13 11 PATIO 4
31 33
34 9 10
32
SUMMERHOUSE 8 7 6

PLANT LIST

1 *Agapanthus* 'Blue Giant'
2 *Pittosporum tenuifolium* 'Irene Paterson'
3 *Clematis* 'Ville de Lyon'
4 *Garrya elliptica* 'James Roof'
5 *Fuchsia* 'Tom Thumb'
6 *Hedera canariensis* 'Gloire de Marengo'
7 *Jasminum nudiflorum*
8 *Clematis alpina* 'Frances Rivis'
9 *Hypericum* 'Hidcote'
10 *Erica erigena* 'Irish Salmon'
11 *Aster novi-belgii* 'Little Pink Beauty'

12 *Phlox paniculata* 'White Admiral'
13 *Vitis vinifera* 'Purpurea'
14 *Actinidia kolomikta*
15 *Hemerocallis* 'Stella de Oro'
16 *Eccremocarpus scaber*
17 *Hydrangea anomala* subsp. *petiolaris*
18 *Rosa* 'Zéphirine Drouhin'
19 *Spiraea japonica* 'Shirobana'
20 *Choisya ternata* 'Sundance'
21 *Lavandula angustifolia* 'Hidcote'
22 *Viola* 'Clementina'
23 *Trachelospermum asiaticum*
24 *Hedera colchica* 'Sulphur Heart'
25 *Jasminum officinale* 'Aureum'
26 *Potentilla fruticosa* 'Abbotswood'
27 *Rudbeckia fulgida* var. *deamii*
28 *Vitis coignetiae*
29 *Hosta* 'Halcyon'
30 *Rosa* 'Golden Showers'
31 *Rosa* 'Paul's Scarlet Climber'
32 *Lonicera periclymenum* 'Serotina'
33 *Aster novi-belgii* 'Lady in Blue'
34 *Miscanthus* 'Silberfeder'
35 *Leucanthemum* × *superbum* 'Snowcap'

GARDEN (long boundaries) 10 x 10m (33 x 33ft)

The underplanting at the base of the climbers consists largely of a mixture of perennials and dwarf shrubs that either have relatively upright flowers and stems, such as *Phlox paniculata* 'White Admiral', or that have a neat, compact habit, including Michaelmas daisy (*Aster novi-belgii* 'Little Pink Beauty') and *Fuchsia* 'Tom Thumb'. Plants of this type are ideally suited to being grown in the comparatively narrow or confined spaces available in this garden.

The features

The dominant feature of the garden is the trellis work itself, which consists of square-patterned panels made out of pressure-treated softwood with curved tops, which create a scalloped effect when they are placed side by side. This woodwork is painted with a cedar-coloured or similar stain to give a warm, light effect when the climbers are dormant and leafless. The panels are secured between matching posts, and there is always the option of fixing ornamental cappings or finials to the tops of the posts for added interest.

The patio is constructed using a warm brown paving brick, which is laid in a basketweave pattern on a sand bed on top of a level hardcore base. Around the edge of the patio, however, the bricks need to be laid on a sand–cement mortar bed to fix them in position and prevent them from creeping sideways into the surrounding borders.

In reality, the cedarwood summerhouse with its shingle roof is included more for appearance than practicality, since it is only a quarter of an octagon. A full-sized summerhouse would encroach much further into the lawn and would be out of proportion to the rest of the garden. It does,

however, serve as a very useful store for garden furniture and the like.

On the opposite side of the lawn to the summerhouse, the stepping-stone path leading from the patio to the utility area consists of buff, 45cm (18in) square, concrete flagstones, which are let into and just below the level of the lawn. In this way a perfectly practical path is provided that does not break up the overall shape of the lawn.

Paving in and around the utility area uses the same type of flag as the stepping stone path, but in this case a larger size of square, 60cm (2ft), is selected. This paving acts not only as a path to the back door and around the sides of the kitchen garden but also serves as a base for a small garden shed and a greenhouse on the far side.

VARIATIONS

▶ Wide, shallow variation

The garden is divided into two main areas to provide a worthwhile lawn space. The other half is then divided diagonally to accommodate the patio and utility area, which allows a naturally flowing link between all three.

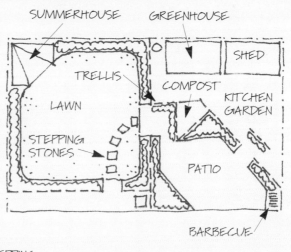

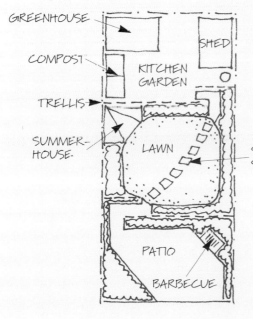

◀ Long, narrow variation

The trellis panels are used in a traditional way to break up the narrowness of the plot by creating three separate spaces, which are linked by paths and stepping stones.

Front Garden

The design

Front gardens, as a rule, differ from back gardens in two basic respects. First, they are unlikely to be used in the same way for general leisure and relaxation as a back garden. Second, they will be open to view, if not to the public at large then certainly to any callers to the house, and they will, therefore, be more open to scrutiny.

The ideal front garden might be one that creates an attractive, inviting entrance to the house yet requires virtually no upkeep, so that most of your valuable gardening or leisure time can be spent in the back garden where it will be best appreciated by you and your family.

This design for a small, narrow front garden relies on the boldness and simplicity of a circular motif of brick, gravel and stone, which not only makes a striking feature but also diverts attention away from the shape and size of the plot. For added interest, the path cuts diagonally across the garden from the pavement to the front door – rather than just straight up the middle or down one side – curving as it does around a sundial placed as a focal point in the centre.

The area between the brick circle and the boundary fencing is planted with varieties that are ideal for use as ground cover and require little attention, and a small tree, set in one corner near the pavement, gives some valuable height and scale to the design. Along the front of the house is a gravel strip, which acts as an access path for maintenance and window-cleaning, and on which containers of annual bedding or other plants can be placed at various times of the year to add extra splashes of colour and interest.

The planting

Low maintenance is one of the priorities of this design and so the planting consists of a mixture of shrubs and perennials that are chosen not only for that purpose but also to provide individual interest at different times of the year and to create an overall composition that is very appealing.

Evergreens are particularly valuable in this kind of garden. Some, such as *Viburnum tinus* 'Purpureum' and *Escallonia* 'Apple Blossom', are selected to give height at the back of the beds, while others, such as *Euonymus fortunei* 'Emerald Gaiety' and *Euphorbia amygdaloides* var. *robbiae*, act as low edging towards the front of the borders

In very small gardens, the number of plant varieties is going to be necessarily limited simply because of lack of space, and so each one must provide value for money. Plants with long flowering periods are extremely useful, and here *Potentilla fruticosa* 'Tilford Cream' and *P. f.* 'Elizabeth' and winter-flowering heathers, such as *Erica × darleyensis* 'Silberschmelze' and *E. carnea* 'Myretoun Ruby', fit the bill exactly.

Plants with a shorter flowering time but that have the added attraction of coloured or variegated foliage are also of great value. *Iris foetidissima* 'Variegata', which has variegated foliage, and *Berberis thunbergii* 'Atropurpurea Nana', which has purple foliage, are good examples of this.

Juniper (*Juniperus chinensis* 'Pyramidalis') and *Miscanthus sinensis* var. *purpurascens* are included for their upright habit, which provides a contrast to some of the lower plants, as well as their own individually attractive foliage effects.

As a final touch, to further emphasize the circular theme and at the same time to provide a softening effect to the hard edge of the paving, there is a low hedge of *Euonymus fortunei* 'Emerald 'n' Gold' enclosing the centre stone circle where it meets the gravel surround.

Changing the direction of a path through angles or curves is a very striking and effective way of providing interest in a small garden.

The features

The edge of the large outer circle is defined by charcoal grey paving bricks laid stretcher bond (end to end) on a bed of sand–cement mortar on top of a narrow base of either well-compacted hardcore or lean concrete (made from about 1 part cement to 10–12 parts ballast). The joints between the bricks are pointed with the same mortar to eliminate gaps where weed seeds might settle and grow. This same brick edge construction is also used to define and separate the narrow gravel access strip next to the house from the back of the shrub border which is adjacent to it.

PLANTING PLAN

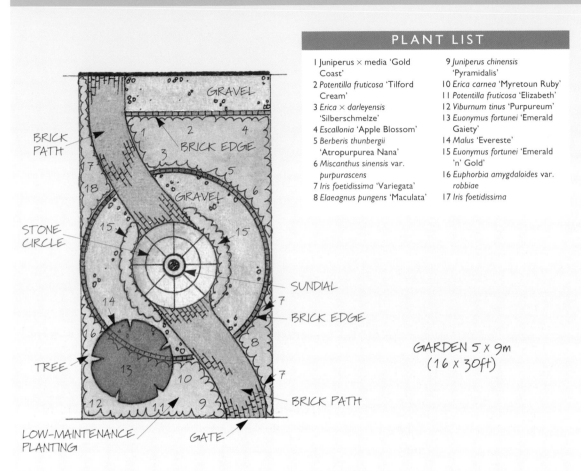

BRICK
PATH

BRICK EDGE

GRAVEL

STONE
CIRCLE

SUNDIAL

BRICK EDGE

TREE

BRICK PATH

LOW-MAINTENANCE
PLANTING

GATE

GRAVEL

GRAVEL

GARDEN 5 x 9m
(16 x 30ft)

PLANT LIST

1 Juniperus × media 'Gold Coast'
2 Potentilla fruticosa 'Tilford Cream'
3 Erica × darleyensis 'Silberschmelze'
4 Escallonia 'Apple Blossom'
5 Berberis thunbergii 'Atropurpurea Nana'
6 Miscanthus sinensis var. purpurascens
7 Iris foetidissima 'Variegata'
8 Elaeagnus pungens 'Maculata'

9 Juniperus chinensis 'Pyramidalis'
10 Erica carnea 'Myretoun Ruby'
11 Potentilla fruticosa 'Elizabeth'
12 Viburnum tinus 'Purpureum'
13 Euonymus fortunei 'Emerald Gaiety'
14 Malus 'Evereste'
15 Euonymus fortunei 'Emerald 'n' Gold'
16 Euphorbia amygdaloides var. robbiae
17 Iris foetidissima

In contrast, the path across the garden consists of red bricks, also laid stretcher bond, with the two outer edges constructed in the same way as the brick circle to act as restraints so that the infill bricks between them require only to be laid on a sand bed on top of a hardcore base.

At the centre of the garden is a circle made up of identical wedge-shaped sections of concrete, pre-cast to imitate natural stone. These are available in packs, each pack making a circular area of paving and leaving a small circular space in the centre, which here is occupied by a sundial, but could just as easily be taken up by a different type of ornament or statue, or possibly even a small, slow-growing tree such as a golden honey locust (*Gleditsia triacanthos* 'Sunburst').

A pale creamy-brown gravel is used to infill the area within the brick circle and also for the access strip immediately in front of the house. The gravel is laid on top of a proprietary landscape fabric or even

VARIATIONS

▶ Wide, shallow variation

The main gravel circle runs right up to the house wall, thus keeping the proportions of planting the same. It combines with the access strip, but is still defined by a brick edging.

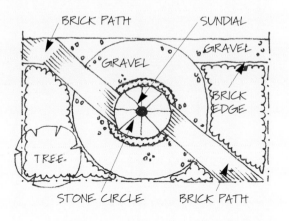

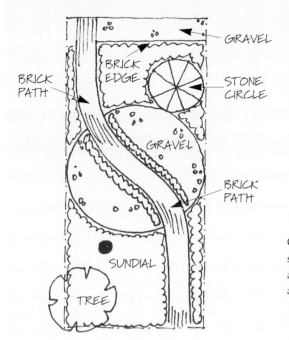

◀ Long, narrow variation

Greater interest is provided by separating the elements of sundial, gravel circle and stone circle to form a diagonal axis – together with the tree – which runs counter to the axis of the brick path.

on heavy duty black polythene – as long as it is punctured to allow some drainage   to provide an effective and attractive weed-free foil to the plants and paving around it.

Although the plants selected for the borders will eventually provide an effective ground cover once they are established, a mulch of coarse, dark bark chippings – ideally at least 5cm (2in) deep – will be equally effective in the short term while the plants are maturing.

Bark chippings have the added advantages of looking attractive and of helping to reduce moisture loss from the soil surface during hot, dry spells.

Index of Plants

Page references in *italics* are to captions

General Index

Page references in *italics* are to captions

Acknowledgements

PHOTOGRAPHS

Jerry Harpur 2 (designer: John Plummer, London), 9 (designer: John Plummer, London), 27 (designer: John Plummer, London), 31 (designer: Simon Fraser, Middlesex), 47 (designer: Judith Sharpe, Clapham), 63 (designer: John Plummer, London), 75 (designer: Edwina von Gal, New York);

Marcus Harpur 7 (Gages, Good Easter, Essex);

Andrew Lawson 1, 8 (designer: Jonathan Baillie), 15 (designer: Andy Rees), 19, 39, 43, 55, 59, 67 (designer: Pattie Barron), 71 (Owl Cottage, Isle of Wight), 83;

Clive Nichols 6 (designers: Andrew and Karla Newell), 11 (designer: Stephen Woodhams), 23 (designers: Clive and Jane Nichols), 35 (White Windows, Hampshire), 51 (designer: Rani Lall), 79 (designers: Andrew and Karla Newell), 87 (designer: Jean Bishop).

ARTWORK

Tim Newbury Plans and line artwork.

Ann Winterbotham Colour artwork.